# In Ruins

*For Michael and Isabel Briggs*

# In Ruins

## Christopher Woodward

*Pantheon Books, New York*

All rights reserved under International and Pan-American
Copyright Conventions. Published in the United States by
Pantheon Books, a division of Random House, Inc., New York.
Originally published in Great Britain by Chatto & Windus,
London, in 2001.

Pantheon Books and colophon are registered trademarks
of Random House, Inc.

Grateful acknowledgment is made for permission to reprint an
excerpt from *The Rings of Saturn*, by W. G. Sebald. First published
by Vito von Eichborn Verlag under the title *Die Ringe des Saturn*,
in 1995. Copyright © Vito von Eichborn Verlag, Frankfurt am
Main. English translation first published by The Harvill Press in
1998. English translation copyright © 1998 by Michael Hulse.
Reprinted by permission of The Harvill Press.

Library of Congress Cataloging-in-Publication Data
Woodward, Christopher.
In ruins / Christopher Woodward.
p.   cm.
ISBN 0-375-42199-8
1. Ruins—Anecdotes. 2. Ruins—Social aspects—Anecdotes.
3. Historic sites—Anecdotes. 4. Voyages and travels—Anecdotes.
5. Artists—Travel—Anecdotes. 6. Authors—Journeys—
Anecdotes. 7. Travelers' writings. I. Title.
CC175.W66 2002   930.1—dc21   2002022019

www.pantheonbooks.com

Printed in the United States of America
First American Edition

2 4 6 8 9 7 5 3 1

# Contents

For I know some will say, why does he treat us
to descriptions of weeds, and make us hobble
after him over broken stones, decayed buildings,
and old rubbish?

Preface to *A Journey into Greece*
by George Wheeler (1682)

# In Ruins

# Who Killed Daisy Miller?

In the closing scene of *Planet of the Apes* (1968) Charlton Heston, astronaut, rides away into the distance. 'What will he find out there?' asks one ape. 'His destiny,' replies another. On a desolate seashore a shadow falls across Heston's figure. He looks up, then tumbles from his horse in bewilderment. 'Oh my God! I'm back. I'm home. Damn you all to hell! . . . You maniacs. They did it, they finally did it, they blew it up!' The shadow is cast by the Statue of Liberty. She is buried up to her waist, her tablet battered, and her torch fractured. The planet of the apes is Earth, he realises, destroyed by a nuclear holocaust while the astronauts were travelling in space. He is the last man, and the lone and level sands stretch far away.

A century before the film was made, a man in a black cape sits on the arch of a ruined bridge. He holds an artist's sketchbook as firmly as if inscribing an epitaph. Blackened shells of buildings rise at the marshy edge of a slow and reedy river, one façade advertising 'COMMERCIAL WHARF'. This is London – or, rather, its future as imagined by the artist Gustave Doré in 1873. The wizard-like figure in Doré's engraving is a traveller from New Zealand, for to many Victorians this young colony seemed to represent the dominant civilisation of the future. He sits on a broken arch of London Bridge to sketch the ruins of St Paul's, exactly as

Victorian Englishmen sketched those of ancient Rome. The cathedral-like ruin next to the commercial warehouse is Cannon Street Station, brand-new in 1873 but here imagined with the cast-iron piers of the bridge rusting away in the tidal ooze.

*The New Zealander* by Gustave Doré, from *London*, 1873.

When we contemplate ruins, we contemplate our own future. To statesmen, ruins predict the fall of Empires, and to philosophers the futility of mortal man's aspirations. To a poet, the decay of a monument represents the dissolution of the individual ego in the flow of Time; to a painter or architect, the fragments of a stupendous antiquity call into question the purpose of their art. Why struggle with a brush or chisel to create the beauty of wholeness when far greater works have been destroyed by Time?

Some years ago I was walking through the Rijksmuseum in Amsterdam, past Rembrandt's *Nightwatch* and into the rooms of hunters, skaters and merry peasants painted during the Golden Age of the Netherlands. I was brought up short by a small, dark painting which hung ignored by the crowds: a view of the interior of an artist's studio painted in the middle of the seventeenth century by a man named Michiel Sweerts. The background of the scene was absolutely predictable: in the convention of artists' academies, students were drawing an antique sculpture of a naked figure, while an older artist was casting a figure in bronze.

In the foreground, however, fragments of ancient statues of gods and heroes formed a gleaming pile of marble rubble, painted with such a heightened degree of illumination and clarity that they seemed to be a collage of photographs cut out and pasted on to the canvas. I was mesmerised by this picture, as unsettled as if I had rediscovered a forgotten nightmare. My mind travelled on to the fragmentary figures in de Chirico's surrealist paintings, and to the pallid flesh of more recent butcheries. On the left of the pile, I now noticed, was the head of a man wearing a turban, as artists did in their studios. Was this a self-portrait of Sweerts? I had never heard of him, a painter who was born in Brussels in 1618 and who died in Goa at the age of forty. Did he kill himself, for a kind of suicide is implied by the painting? There was no more information on the label but I was convinced that, at the very least, he abandoned his career as a painter. The clash of creativity and destruction in this

*The Artist's Studio* by Michiel Sweerts, *c*.1640.

canvas expressed the inner doubts of an artist confronted by the stupendous classical past but, ironically, the promise of ruin has been one of the greatest inspirations to western art.

When I turned away from Sweerts's studio, I felt oddly dislocated but also very calm. Why, I wondered, does immersion in ruins instill such a lofty, even ecstatic, drowsiness? Samuel Johnson spoke of how 'Whatever withdraws us from the power of our senses – whatever makes the past, the distant, or the future, predominate over the present, advances us in the dignity of human beings. . . . That man is little to be envied, whose patriotism would not gain force upon the plains of Marathon, or whose enthusiasm would not grow warmer among the ruins of Rome.' Sweerts had been to Rome, I was sure. For it is the shadow of classical antiquity which is the deepest source for the fascination with ruins in the western world. Every new empire has claimed to be the heir of Rome, but if such a colossus as Rome can crumble – its ruins ask – why not London or New York? Furthermore, the magnitude of its ruins overturned visitors' assumptions about the inevitability of human progress over Time. London in Queen Victoria's reign was the first European city to exceed ancient Rome in population and in geographical extent; until the Crystal Palace was erected in Hyde Park in 1851, the Colosseum (or Coliseum) remained the largest architectural volume in existence. Any visitor to Rome in the fifteen centuries after its sack by the Goths in AD 410 would have experienced that strange sense of displacement which occurs when we find that, living, we cannot fill the footprints of the dead.

A second shadow falls on the same ground. This is the Christian doctrine that man's achievement on earth is a fleeting transience, that pyramids and houses and skyscrapers will crumble into oblivion at the sound of the Last Trump. The apocalyptic finale is not exclusive to the Christian religion, but what is unique is the conjunction of the cult's holy shrines with the greatest ruins of classical civilisation. The two greatest influences on the mind of Europe share the same circle of hills above the River Tiber. So the Eternal City is the place to begin an investigation into the feelings of pleasure and fear which ruins suggest.

In AD 400 Rome was a city of eight hundred thousand people glittering with 3,785 statues of gold, marble and

bronze. Its encircling walls were 10 miles in length with 376
towers, and vaulted by nineteen aqueducts carrying fresh
spring-water to 1,212 drinking fountains and 926 public
baths. There is no evidence that any writer or painter
imagined its future ruin, and the poet Rutilius Namatianus
expressed his contemporaries' view that Rome was as eternal
as the universe itself:

> No man will ever be safe if he forgets you;
> May I praise you still when the sun is dark.
> To count up the glories of Rome is like counting
> The stars in the sky.

In AD 410 the Visigoths seized and plundered the city, and
in 455 the Ostrogoths. By the end of that century only a
hundred thousand citizens remained in Rome, and the rich
had fled to Constantinople or joined the Goths in their new
capital at Ravenna. In the sixth century the Byzantines and
the Goths contested the city three times and the population
fell to thirty thousand, clustered in poverty beside the River
Tiber now that the aqueducts had been destroyed and the
drinking fountains were dry. The fall of Rome came to be
seen by many as the greatest catastrophe in the history of
western civilisation.

In architectural terms, however, change was slow. The
Goths plundered but they did not burn or destroy. In the
words of St Jerome, 'The Gods adored by nations are now
alone in their niches with the owls and the night-birds. The
gilded Capitol languishes in dust and all the temples of
Rome are covered with spiders' webs.' The public buildings
on the Capitoline Hill and the Forum were abandoned

while a new city, Christian Rome, rose around the outlying sites of St Peter's martyrdom and the Pope's palace of St John Lateran. Over the centuries the Forum became a cow pasture, and cattle drank in the fountains where Castor and Pollux were said to have watered their sweating steeds after the battle of Lake Regillus. Debris slid down the steep slope of the Capitoline Hill to bury the Temple of Vespasian in a mound 33 feet deep. Four-fifths of the vast area enclosed by the old fortified walls of Rome became a wasteland scattered with ruins, vineyards and farms. It remained *disabitato* until after 1870, when the city became the capital of a reunited nation, the 'third Rome'.

But if the Goths did not demolish the buildings, where did the dusty, cobwebbed temples disappear to? They were recycled: in the thousand years that followed, ancient Rome was remade as Christian Rome. In the darkness of the deserted ruins the colonnades echoed with the clang of mallets as thieves stole the gold and bronze statues in order to melt them down. And why open a quarry when the Forum was on the new city's doorstep, with its stones polished and ready? The Colosseum was leased as a quarry by the Popes: picking up one receipt in the Vatican archive we see a payment of 205 ducats for the removal of 2,522 tons of stone between September 1451 and May 1452. One of the first Popes to introduce legislation to protect the few monuments that still stood was Pius II, in 1462. A humanist scholar, Pius had praised the ruins in a poem written many years before:

> Oh Rome! Your very ruins are a joy,
> Fallen is your pomp; but it was peerless once!

Your noble blocks wrench'd from your ancient walls
Are burn'd for lime by greedy slaves of gain.
Villains! If such as you may have their way
Three ages more, Rome's glory will be gone.

Pius's laws were disregarded like many before or since, however. In 1519 Raphael told Pope Leo X, 'I would be so bold as to say that all of this new Rome, however great it may be, however beautiful, however embellished with palaces, churches and other buildings, all of this is built with mortar made from ancient marbles.' In the twelve years since Raphael had known the city the Temple of Ceres and one of its two pyramids had been destroyed. The lime-burning which Pius II and Raphael decried was the most banal, yet most destructive, aspect of the recycling. In mixing mortar the best aggregate is powdered lime, and the easiest way to obtain powdered lime is to burn marble. At the end of the nineteenth century the archaeologist Rodolfo Lanciani discovered a lime-kiln abandoned by lime-burners in a sudden hurry many centuries before. Inside stood eight marble Vestal Virgins ready to be burned, stashed 'like a cord of wood, leaving as few interstices as possible between them, and the spaces formed by the curves of the body filled in by marble chips'. Once when he was sketching in the Forum, the great French seventeenth-century painter Nicolas Poussin was asked where to find the spirit of ancient Rome. He knelt down and scooped up a handful of earth. 'Here.' The cow pasture was mingled with marble dust, the richest sediment in the world.

From the fall of classical Rome until the eighteenth century the only houses in the Forum were the cottages of

The Roman Forum by Giovanni Battista Piranesi, *c.*1751. At the fall of Rome, the Forum was abandoned to the lime-burners and to cattle; in the eighteenth century, it continued to be called the *Campo Vaccino*, or cow pasture.

the lime-burners, and the hovels of beggars and thieves. To Christian pilgrims in the Middle Ages the ruins were the work of mysterious giants of folklore and not fellow men, and the Colosseum was thought to have been a domed Temple of the Sun. The marshy, fetid wilderness of the Forum was to be avoided in the journey from one shrine to another. A soldier in the army of Frederick Barbarossa which invaded Rome in 1155 described the ruins crawling with green snakes and black toads, its air poisoned by the breath of winged dragons, and by the rotting bodies of the thousands of Germans who had died of the fever during their occupation of the city. When Adam of Usk travelled from Henry V's England he saw dogs scrapping outside St Peter's: 'O God! How lamentable is the state of Rome! Once it was filled by great Lords and Palaces; now it's filled with huts, thieves, wolves and vermin, and the Romans tear themselves to pieces.'

It was not until the Renaissance of the fifteenth century that we find a new approach, in which the study of ancient inscriptions and manuscripts replaced superstitious legends, and artists and architects tried to piece together the scattered jigsaws of antiquity. The first painting of the ruins of the Forum was made by Maso di Banco in the church of Santa Croce in Florence in 1336, and at the dawn of the following century Brunelleschi and Donatello came from Florence to study the remains. When they began to excavate, the local rabble assumed they were treasure-hunters; when they used compasses and rulers to establish the measurements they needed for their own works of art they were accused of being necromancers using occult secrets to discover the gold and silver. The antiquary Poggio Bracciolini arrived in Rome in 1430:

> The hill of the Capitol, on which we sit, was formerly
> the head of the Roman Empire, the citadel of the earth,
> the terror of kings; illustrated by the footsteps of so
> many triumphs, enriched with the spoils and tributes of
> so many nations. This spectacle of the world, how it is
> fallen! How changed! How defaced! The path of victory
> is obliterated by vines, and the benches of the senators
> are concealed by a dunghill. . . . The Forum of the

Roman people, where they assembled to enact their
laws and elect their magistrates, is now enclosed for the
reception of swine and buffaloes. The public and private
edifices, that were founded for eternity, lie prostrate,
broken, and naked, like the limbs of a mighty giant; and
the ruin is the more visible, from the stupendous relics
that have survived the injuries of time and fortune.

Poggio's lament became a new way of seeing Rome. And
nowhere was the lesson of *Sic transit gloria mundi* more
evident than in the Colosseum. It had served as a quarry, a
private fortress and a bull-ring: earthquakes had struck in
422, 508, 847, 1231 and 1349 AD. Its external arcades,
littered with dunghills, were full of beggars and occupied by
shopkeepers who slung their awnings on poles slotted into
the holes where clamps of bronze had once held the marble
cladding in place. Even inside you could smell the cabbages
from the surrounding farms.

> Quamdiu stat Colyseus, stat et Roma:
> Quando cadet Colyseus, cadet et Roma:
> Quando cadet Roma, cadet et Mundus.

As Byron translated the words of the Venerable Bede:

> While stands the Coliseum, Rome shall stand
> When falls the Coliseum, Rome shall fall
> And when Rome falls – the world.

It is oval in plan, 617 feet in length and 513 feet in width
and 187 feet high. The arena was built by Emperor Vespasian

and opened in AD 80, when it was welcomed as 'the eighth wonder of the world' by the poet Martial. It contained fifty thousand spectators. For naval battles the arena was flooded, and when gladiators fought lions, panthers, elephants and ostriches it was redecorated as a jungle or a rocky desert. Christians were fed to the lions from the earliest days of the arena, and it was they who banned the gladiatorial games in AD 404.

The Christian Emperor Constantine had deliberately placed the principal Christian shrines – such as St Peter's and the Lateran Palace – at a discreet distance from the temples of the classical gods. In the Colosseum a clash of the two religions was unavoidable, however, and the sand impregnated with the blood of martyrs became a place of pilgrimage. At the beginning of the eighteenth century it was formally consecrated to the martyrs, and pilgrims processed round the Stations of the Cross erected at the rim of the arena, or kissed the tall black cross in the centre for 100 days' indulgence. The more intrepid pilgrims climbed the tangled, slippery terraces to plant crosses at the grassy summit. A hermitage was built into the tiers of the amphitheatre; one occupant was fined for selling hay he had grown in the arena. The Colosseum showed the Romans at their mightiest but also at their cruellest, so a visit was a dilemma for any Christian with a classical education. The ambivalence is best expressed by Charles Dickens in his *Letters from Italy* (1846). The faces of Italians changed as he entered Rome:

> beauty becomes devilish; and there is scarcely one
> countenance in a hundred, among the common people

in the streets, that would not be at home and happy in a
renovated Coliseum to-morrow. . . . [Inside the arena]
its solitude, its awful beauty, and its utter desolation,
strike upon the stranger, the next moment, like a
softened sorrow; and never in his life, perhaps, will he
be so moved and overcome by any sight, not
immediately connected with his own affections and
afflictions.

   To see it crumbling there, an inch a year; its walls and
arches overgrown with green; its corridors open to the
day; the long grass growing in its porches; young trees
of yesterday, springing up on its ragged parapets, and
bearing fruit: chance produce of the seeds dropped
there by the birds who build their nests within its chinks
and crannies; to see its Pit of Fight filled up with earth,
and the peaceful Cross planted in the centre; to climb
into its upper halls, and look down on ruin, ruin, ruin,
all about it . . . is to see the ghost of old Rome, wicked
wonderful old city, haunting the very ground on which
its people trod. It is the most impressive, the most
stately, the most solemn, grand, majestic, mournful
sight, conceivable. Never, in its bloodiest prime, can the
sight of the gigantic Coliseum, full and running over
with the lustiest life, have moved one heart, as it must
move all who look upon it now, a ruin. GOD be
thanked: a ruin!

   The very opposite view is given by William Beckford who
came to Rome in the autumn of 1779, in the heyday of the
Grand Tour. With an inheritance of £1 million in Jamaican
sugar 'England's wealthiest son' – in Byron's phrase – was

perhaps the most marvellously spoiled figure in the history
of English arts. Taught music by Mozart at the age of five –
when the composer was seven – he wrote the oriental
romance *Vathek* at the age of twenty-one. After a homo-
sexual scandal with a young aristocrat he was banished from
society for the next sixty years, and he erected in Wiltshire
the mock-Gothic abbey of Fonthill as a private temple of the
arts. We have an inkling of Fonthill's decadent, theatrical
interiors in his response to St Peter's, which he entered the
moment his retinue of carriages arrived in Rome. Banish the
priests, he wrote to a confidante, and you and I could live in
a tent draped over Bernini's bronze baldacchino below the
dome. Drape yellow silk over the windows and we will for-
get the passing of days, the oil lamps in their niches, the stars
in an endless night. It required an arrogant imagination to
claim St Peter's as a private hermitage – and a mischievous
anti-clericalism.

Reaching the Colosseum his impulse was to kick the tacky
clutter of martyrdom into the river. 'A few lazy abbots were
at their devotions before [the Stations of the Cross], such as
would have made a lion's mouth water, fatter, I dare say,
than any saint in the whole martyrology, and ten times more
tantalising.' In the seclusion of cypresses growing in an
arcade he conjured up in his mind the colourful din of an
ancient Roman triumph, before wandering into the Forum.
On the Palatine Hill beyond, only the cellars remained of the
palaces built by the Caesars, and under one arch a 'wretched
rabble' of beggars roasted wild chestnuts. Beckford observed
the lessons of this tableau until the fire died 'and none
remained but a withered hag, raking the embers and muttering to herself' like a witch of old. But the autumn mists

which streamed through the apertures of the Colosseum had given him a headache and he returned to his hotel.

In the eighteenth century many Grand Tourists shared Beckford's Enlightenment disgust for the Catholic clergy and their institutions, while Dickens was addressing a more pious High Victorian audience. The change in religious culture is not the point, however: I choose the Colosseum to show how ruins inspire such a variety of responses. Each spectator is forced to supply the missing pieces from his or her own imagination and a ruin therefore appears different to everyone. It is an obvious point perhaps; it first struck me when visiting Captain Coram's Foundling Hospital in London, which displays the 'tokens' that accompanied the children who were placed on the doorstep by their anonymous mothers. A token was an object snapped in two, whether a gold ring or a porcelain plate, and only by reuniting the two imperfect halves could a mother reclaim her child. But what fantasies of family did each abandoned child project on to its fragment?

As if to illustrate this dialogue between incompleteness and the imagination, the most powerful response to the arena is by Edgar Allan Poe – a writer who never set foot in Italy. His poem 'The Coliseum' was published in the *Baltimore Saturday Visitor* of 26 October 1833, the week after the young and unknown journalist had published his first prize-winning short story. Later, Poe incorporated the poem into *Politian*, his one attempt at a drama in verse. The play translated to Renaissance Rome the recent scandal of a love-triangle in Frankfort, Kentucky, when a jealous attorney stabbed to death a politician who had earlier fathered a child by his fiancée. The poem became a soliloquy spoken by the hero of *Politian* as he awaits his lover in the moonlit Colosseum. Beginning with the old refrain of *Sic transit gloria mundi* – 'Here where the dames of Rome their yellow hair / Waved to the wind, now wave the reed and thistle' – the lover's own voice rises to address the echoing ring of stone.

> These stones, alas! These grey stones are they all
> Of the great and colossal left
> By the corrosive hours to fate and me?

The stones echo a reply:

> . . . Prophetic sounds and loud arise forever
> From us and from all ruin unto the wise,
> As from the granite Memnon to the sun.
> We rule the hearts of mightiest men: we rule
> With a despotic sway all giant minds.
> We are not desolate we pallid stones,
> Not all our power is gone – not all our Fame
> Not all the magic of our high renown
> Not all the wonder that encircles us
> Not all the mysteries that in us lie
> Not all the memories that hang upon
> And cling around about us as a garment
> Clothing us in a robe of more than glory.

We understand Poe's symbolism by turning to the story he published in the same magazine the previous week. Entitled 'MS Found in a Bottle' it is narrated by a man whose cynicism is as expensive as William Beckford's: 'all my life I have been a dealer in antiquities, and have imbibed the shadows of fallen columns at Balbac, and Tadmor, and Persepolis, until my very soul has become a ruin. . . .' The antique dealer is rescued at sea by a ghostly vessel, made of some porous but ageless wood and crewed by somnambulant, ethereal sailors. 'The ship and all in it are imbued with the spirit of Eld', he notes. They drift towards destruction at the South Pole, which Poe imagined as an open spinning vortex of eternity, its walls of ice 'a gigantic amphitheatre, the summit of whose walls is lost in the darkness and the distance'.

The roaring circle of ice and the Colosseum are both 'Eld', a swirling infinity that was Poe's concept of eternity. In an age of scientific progress Poe was an anti-Positivist; that is, as he wrote to a friend: 'I disagree with you in what you say of man's advance towards perfection. Man is now only more active, not wiser, nor more happy than he was 6,000 years ago.' In his one non-fiction essay 'Eureka', he argued that the universe could not be quantified by physics or astronomy but was 'a shadowy and fluctuating domain, now shrinking, now swelling, in accordance with the vacillating energies of the imagination'. As Poe studied engravings of the Colosseum – perhaps Piranesi's mesmerising bird's-eye view – he saw not an assembly of stones but a pulsating source of eternal, magical energy.

Its spirit was thrillingly alive for Benvenuto Cellini (1500–71), the Renaissance sculptor and goldsmith who worked for the Popes and King François I of France but is perhaps as celebrated for his lusty autobiography as for his exquisite bronzes. Furious that a teenage Sicilian girl has slipped through his fingers, he hires a necromancer to

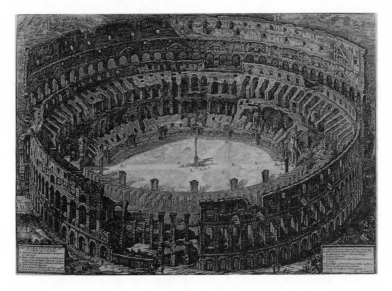

*The Colosseum* by Piranesi, *c.*1751. In Piranesi's bird's eye view, the amphitheatre seems to be the achievement of giants, not men – or, like a volcano, a phenomenon of Nature. The engraving also shows the martyrs' cross in the centre, and, at the edge of the arena, the Stations of the Cross and the hermitage.

summon the spirits that will call her back. Cellini and his friend Angelo meet the magician in the centre of the arena, drawing magic circles in the sand, pouring perfume in the fire and spinning the pentacle until the dark tiers of seats fill with the ghosts of legionaries. In Angelo's eyes the soldiers become demons growing in size and brightness. 'These creatures are only our slaves; all you can see is smoke and shadow!' Cellini calls, but now Angelo sees the entire amphitheatre on fire and flames rushing towards them. In terror, he farts – and Cellini's laughter sends the demons scurrying back into the shadows.

The necromancers lit their fire where the black Martyrs' Cross would later be erected, and on the steps of this cross took place one of the saddest scenes in the autobiography of François-René, Vicomte de Chateaubriand. Architectural ruin was the favourite metaphor of this novelist, traveller and statesman, who was born in a crumbling ancestral castle in Brittany in 1768 and was to see his family guillotined and the châteaux and abbeys of *ancien régime* France plundered and burned in the Revolution. When he returned to Paris from exile in 1800 the Place de la Concorde 'had the decay, the melancholy and deserted look of an old amphitheatre' and he hastened past, chilled by the ghosts of his family and the imagined stains of blood on the paving stones. The saddest memento returned to him was the wedding ring of his sister-in-law, its two inscribed hoops broken in half.

The vicomte was restored to favour by Napoleon and dispatched to Rome, and it was the city's promise of oblivion that inspired him to begin his memoirs. His lover Pauline de Beaumont followed from Paris, although she was dying from tuberculosis. She summoned the energy to leave her lodgings for the last time, and expressed her wish to kneel at the Martyrs' Cross in the Colosseum. Her prayers finished, she raised her eyes to the rim of the arena and to the oval of blue sky above. '"Let us go: I am cold" . . . she went to bed and rose no more.' In S. Luigi de' Francesi, the French church by the Piazza Navona with the Caravaggios, is the beautiful memorial he erected to her memory.

Did the romantic egotist theatricalise the episode? Probably, but the arena demanded drama of its visitors. Its sand was as resonant as the wooden planking of the stage, and at night its empty stalls were a hushed, dimmed auditorium; the Colosseum had the loudest echo in the world. On a night of bright moonlight in 1787 Goethe watched the beggars who had bivouacked under the arches light a fire in the centre, and the phenomenon of the smoke swirling around the bowl gave rise to one of the most celebrated visions in *The Italian Journey* (1816):

> Presently the smoke found its way up the sides, and
> through every chink and opening, while the moon lit it
> up like a cloud. The sight was exceedingly glorious. In
> such a light one ought also to see the Pantheon, the
> Capitol, the Portico of St Peter's, and the grand streets
> and squares. And thus the sun and the moon, as well as
> the human mind, have here to do a work quite different
> from what they produce elsewhere – here where vast
> and yet elegant masses present themselves to their rays.

Perversely, Henry James used the arena's amplification to place in scale the littleness of human transactions. It is here that he set the final act of his 1878 novella, *Daisy Miller*. At eleven o'clock in the evening Nigel Winterbourne is wandering through the city struggling to clarify his confusions over Daisy, a capricious American heiress. When he enters the arena his first response is to murmur the lines from Byron's drama *Manfred*, which had become the most celebrated description to nineteenth-century tourists:

> When I was wandering, – upon such a night
> I stood within the Coliseum's wall,
> Midst the chief relics of almighty Rome!
> The trees which grew along the broken arches

Waved dark in the blue midnight, and the stars
Shone through the rents of ruin; from afar
The watchdog bay'd beyond the Tiber; and
More near from out the Caesars' palace came
The owl's long cry . . .
Ivy usurps the laurel's place of growth; –
But the gladiators' bloody Circus stands,
A noble wreck in ruinous perfection!

The Colosseum is filled with mist, a miasma released into the air by recent excavations in the sewers. Seated at the base of the cross are Daisy and Giovanelli, a handsome Italian who is his sly rival. For Winterbourne the composition has a sudden, welcome clarity: 'She was a young lady about the *shades* of whose perversity a foolish puzzled gentleman need no longer trouble his head or heart. That once questionable quantity *had* no shades – it was a mere little black blot.' His mind resolved, he speaks only to instruct her that the miasma is a danger to her health. She protests: 'I never was sick, and I don't mean to be! I don't look like much, but I'm healthy! I was bound to see the Coliseum by moonlight – I wouldn't have wanted to go home without that . . . ' Their last words are exchanged in the tunnel of the entrance as, driving away in a cab, she turns to cry out: 'I don't care whether I have Roman fever or not!' A week later she is dead of malaria.

When the American writer Nathaniel Hawthorne had visited one night twenty years earlier, in 1858, he had been irritated by having to share the stalls with parties of English tourists led by local guides in search of Manfred's sublime solitude, of 'raptures which were Byron's, not their own'.

Hawthorne detested the first 'cold, rainy, filthy, stinking, rotten, rascally' winter in Rome, which he had endured while he worked on the manuscript of *The Marble Faun*: 'I fully acquiesce in all the mischief and ruin that has happened to it, from Nero's conflagration onward. In fact, I wish the very sight had been obliterated before I ever saw it.' His daughter was ill with the fever, and the climate upset his own health: 'I never knew that I had either bowels or lungs before I came to Rome.' Despite this, in *The Marble Faun* he captured the magical atmosphere of summer nights when the guided tours had returned to their hotels and the locals reclaimed the arena:

> Some youths and maidens were running merry races across the open space, and playing at hide-and-seek a little way within the duskiness of the ground-tier of arches; whence, now and then, you could hear the half-shriek, half-laugh of a frolicsome girl, whom the shadow had betrayed into a young man's arms. Elder groups were seated on the fragments of pillars and the blocks of marble, that lie around the verge of this arena, talking in the quick, short ripple of the Italian tongue.

The scene is enjoyed by a group of American artists. 'What a strange thought that the Coliseum was really built for us, and has not come to its best uses till almost two thousand years after it was finished!' comments one. 'The Emperor Vespasian scarcely had us in his mind,' replies another. 'But I thank him none the less for building it.' The conversation precedes a murder, which need not detain us here; nor is there time for the meditations of the poet Shelley or the vision of the chemist Humphry Davy, who saw a spectacle of toppling worlds one starlit night; nor Lamartine's elegy to the sound of the wind whistling through its arches, nor Stendhal's romantic description which he claimed could only be appreciated if read after midnight 'in the house of an amiable woman' with a print illustrating the structure held in one's hand. But no writer saw the same Colosseum.

An English botanist named Richard Deakin in his *Flora of the Colosseum* (1855) gives the most beautiful of all descriptions of the ruin. Deakin catalogued and illustrated no less than 420 species of plants growing in the 6 acres of ruin, a micro-climate which was damp to the north but hot and dry on its southern slopes. There were cypresses and ilex, fifty-six varieties of grass and forty-one of the 'Leguminous or Pea tribe' but Deakin was fondest of the many wild flowers: the dianthus which clustered in the lower arcades, and the star-like anemone which twinkled on the stones in springtime. Some flowers in the Colosseum were so rare in western Europe that the only explanation for their presence was that nearly two thousand years before their seeds had been scattered in the sand from the bodies of animals brought from the mountains of Persia or the banks of the Nile for the gladiatorial games. Deakin's most moving specimen was the discovery of Christ's Thorn, a reminder of the 'eternal crown, without thorns' which each martyr had won. To the sensitive botanist flowers 'form a link in the memory, and teach us hopeful and soothing lessons, amid the sadness of bygone ages: and cold indeed must be the heart that does not respond to their silent appeal; for though without speech, they tell us of the regenerating power which animates the dust of mouldering greatness'.

Fifteen years later every tree was gone, every flower and blade of grass plucked from the ruins by cold-hearted archaeologists. In 1870 control of the ruins was handed over to the archaeologists by the new government which had unified Italy. 'Rome or death!' had been Garibaldi's cry. Cannon-fire at the ancient city gates at dawn on 20 September 1870 announced the end of the Pope's temporal authority and the inauguration of the 'third Rome'. As the windows in the Vatican rattled Pope Pius IX capitulated, and withdrew into internal exile inside the palace. The populace welcomed Vittorio Emmanuele II, King of Sardinia, as King of a reunified Italy.

Rome was to be the capital of a new Italy which would be modern, democratic and secular, its senators in cravats and English suits, and the shining new ministries built on the Tiber humming with elevators and typewriters. The children of their new state would not grow up in a city where the living outnumbered the dead. The Rome of the Middle Ages was now identified with superstition, poverty and civil war, an interlude between the twin pillars of heroic antiquity and the new republic. All relics of this degrading interlude were embarrassments, and several medieval fortified towers were demolished in order to create the podium for the 'wedding cake', the white neo-classical monument on the Capitoline Hill which commemorates King Vittorio Emmanuele. It was precisely this contrast between ancient grandeur and modern squalor, however, which had encouraged visitors from England, France, or America to claim for London, Paris, or New York the right to the title of the 'new Rome', which the wretched natives must surely relinquish. Rome's population doubled from two hundred thousand to four hundred thousand in two decades. The bureaucrats who arrived with the new government required forty thousand office rooms, and modern apartments for their families. Princes sold their homes to property speculators, and palaces like the Villa Ludovisi – Henry James's favourite – were quickly demolished. On the Corso the last empty plot, valued before 1870 at a few centimes, sold for 1,000 francs per square metre. In 1882 Augustus Hare grumbled that 'Twelve years of Sardinian rule have done more for the destruction of Rome . . . than the invasions of the Goths and Vandals'.

The wilderness of pastures, ruins and vineyards inside the city walls disappeared under what Hare described as 'ugly new streets in imitation of Paris and New York', with five-storey stucco apartment blocks as monotonous as barracks. The transformation of the city was described to an English audience by the archaeologist Rodolfo Lanciani in 139 letters to *The Athenaeum* in London published between 1876 and 1913. At first, there was great excitement in removing the layers of medieval detritus to discover the Roman remains underneath. But, by 1887, it was apparent that there had been a price to pay. Rome was no longer

> the Rome of our dreams, of a beautiful brownish hue,
> surrounded by dense masses of green: it is an immense
> white dazzling spot, some six miles in diameter,
> bordering directly on the wilderness of the Campagna
> . . . we miss the aged ilexes, forming as it were the frame
> of the picture, their deep green giving by contrast that
> vigour and brilliancy to the golden hue which old age
> lends to ruins in southern climates . . . we miss that

sense of quiet and peaceful enjoyment which pervaded the whole scene. It is impossible to imagine anything more commonplace, and out of keeping, and shabby, and tasteless, than the new quarters which encircle the city.

In April of 1887 Thomas Hardy and his wife Emma arrived by train from Florence. No writer was more sensitive to the emotional resonance of ruined buildings than this former architect, and in Rome the overpowering spell of decay was 'like a nightmare in my sleep', he wrote. 'How any community can go on building in the face of the Vanitas vanitatum reiterated by the ruins is quite marvellous.' In his poem 'Rome: Building a New Street in the Ancient Quarter' he described the brick and stucco apartment blocks rising in the ruins of 'Time's central city', where the 'cracking frieze and rotten metope' seemed to shout a warning of futility: 'Dunces, Learn here to spell Humanity!'

And yet within these ruins' very shade
The singing workmen shape and set and join
Their frail new mansion's stuccoed cove and quoin
With no apparent sense that years abrade,
Though each rent wall their feeble works invade
Once shamed all such in power of pier and groin.

The Forum came to resemble a 'house-breaker's yard', in the words of one of the many artists who packed up his easel in disgust. But it was the Colosseum which became the flashpoint in the dispute over the true identity of the ruins. Having removed the flowers and trees, in 1874 the archaeologists began to excavate in the arena in order to expose the sewers and cellars. To do so, it was necessary to remove the hermit and his hermitage, the black Martyrs' Cross, and the Stations of the Cross. The Pope emerged from his exile in order to object, and every day processions of Christians came to pray on the sacred sands in protest. The archaeologists withdrew but it was too late: the trenches had filled with water and flooded the arena. It remained a lake for five years, until a new sewer could be constructed. On the day the water drained away, Lanciani told his readers in London, there were loud cheers from the 'crowd assembled to witness the ceremony', perhaps including some of the locals whom Hawthorne had observed. 'Poor Coliseum! It was no longer recognisable since the upsetting of the arena in 1874.' And poor Daisy Miller – it was the excavations that released the fatal vapours from the sewers.

The sewers and underground service corridors have remained exposed ever since, as bald as the foundations of a modern construction site. I cannot find a single writer or painter who has been inspired by the Colosseum since 1870, and only one exception to a general rule: the failed painter, Adolf Hitler, and his architects.

'*Rom hat mich richtig ergriffen!*' ['Rome completely bowled me over!'] His first sight was on a state visit in 1938. Mussolini prepared a ceremonial progression from the railway station at the Pyramid of Caius Cestius to Palazzo Venezia, his palace at the foot of the Capitoline Hill. Hitler's train arrived by night, and the proudest monuments of Imperial Rome were illuminated by 45,000 electric lamps linked by 100 miles of cabling. The Colosseum was lit

Übersicht:

1 Porta S. Paolo
2 Cestius-Pyramide
3 Aventin
4 Serviusmauer
5 S. Balbina
6 Caracalla-Thermen
7 Obelisk von Axum
8 La Vignola
9 S. Gregorio Magno
10 SS. Giovanni e Paolo
11 Palatin
12 Tempel der Venus u. Roma
13 Konstantinsbogen
14 Colosseum
15 Torre dei Conti di Segni
16 Augustus-Forum
17 Trajans-Forum
18 Trajans-Säule
19 Forum Romanum
20 National-Denkmal
21 Cäsar-Forum
22 Palazzo Venezia
23 Quirinal-Palast

Tiber

Ankunfts-Bahnhof.

Rom

Die

Einzugsstraße des

Führers

Nazi Map, 1938. This map records Hitler's journey from the station at Ostia (no. 2) to Mussolini's palace in Palazzo Venezia (no. 22) on his state visit in 1938. The ruins en route were illuminated with 45,000 red lamps.

from inside by red lamps so that, as if ablaze, it cast a bloody glow on to the grass and the ruddy brick ruins on the surrounding slopes. Heavy rain in the days which followed led to military displays being cancelled, and Hitler took the opportunity to return to the Colosseum and spend several hours alone studying designs for the new Congress Hall in Nuremberg. This was amphitheatrical in form: his architect Albert Speer had discussed Goethe's speculation that in the Colosseum the crowd became a single spirit, swaying forward and back in mesmerised loyalty. Hitler saw an even more chilling moral in the structure: the construction of these 'imperishable symbols of power' depended on slaves brought from conquered, 'uncivilised' territories.

On his return to Germany Hitler introduced an official policy, the '*Teorie von Ruinwert*'. Steel and ferro-concrete could no longer be used in the construction of official Nazi buildings because they were too perishable. The use of marble, stone and brick alone would ensure that at the fall of the 1,000-year Reich they would resemble their Roman models. As Speer explained in his memoirs:

> Ultimately, all that remained to remind men of the great epochs of history was their monumental architecture, he recalled. What then remained of the emperors of the Roman Empire? What would still give evidence of them today, if not their buildings. . . . So, today the buildings of ancient Rome could enable Mussolini to refer to the heroic spirit of Rome when he wanted to inspire his people with the idea of a modern imperium. Our buildings must speak to the conscience

of future generations of Germans. With this argument
Hitler also understood the value of a durable kind of
construction.

Speer even presented Hitler with sketches in which he
imagined the marble colonnade of the Zeppelinfeld at
Nuremberg as a romantic, ivy-clad ruin of the future. And in
the Cabinet Room at the Reichstag Hitler hung views of the
Forum painted by the French artist Hubert Robert in the
eighteenth century. Should Hitler's obsession with ruins
deter us from enjoying them ourselves? No; the opposite
rather. To Hitler the Colosseum was not a ruin but a
monument, a bottle that was half-full rather than half-empty
as it were. He was attracted to the endurance of the masonry
and the physical survival of an emperor's ambitions; to the
lover of the ruinous, by contrast, the attraction is in the sight
of transience and vulnerability. Poets and painters like ruins,
and dictators like monuments.

It is for similar reasons that the artist is inevitably at odds
with the archaeologist. In the latter discipline the scattered
fragments of stone are parts of a jigsaw, or clues to a puzzle
to which there is only one answer, as in a science laboratory;
to the artist, by contrast, any answer which is imaginative is
correct. For five centuries the Colosseum nourished artists
and writers, but it was precisely the features which conflicted
with the original 'truth' of the Colosseum which triggered
their creativity. The black Martyrs' Cross, on whose steps sat
Daisy Miller, Chateaubriand and Pauline de Beaumont.
Moonlit solitude, and the owl's cry heard by Byron. The
spectral smoke which drifted away to reveal Cellini's
demons, Goethe's geometries and Poe's dizzying vortex of

Eld. The hermit who grew his hay; William Beckford's reverie in the cypresses; and Deakin's Christ's Thorn. All have gone, and the Colosseum is extinct. Today it is the most monumental bathos in Europe: a bald, dead and bare circle of stones. There are no shadows, no sands, no echoes and if a single flower blooms in a crevice it is sprayed with weed-killer. The monument is open to the public from nine-thirty a.m. to six p.m., when the gates are locked. At nightfall one day in the 1820s Stendhal watched an Englishman ride his horse through the deserted arena. I wish that could be me.

## II

# A Perverse Pleasure

'I was born in Avila, the old city of the walls', wrote the Spanish novelist Miguel Delibes in his novel of 1948, *The Shadow of the Cypress Is Lengthening*. Avila is a city high on the bare plateau west of Madrid, admired for its unbroken circuit of medieval fortifications. Today it prospers on tourists visiting the convent of St Teresa and buying trinkets in narrow streets that seem to have changed little since her time. Fifty years ago, however, half the area within the walls was derelict and abandoned, and the granite doorways were silent: no radios playing, no children, only the footsteps of widows and saints. The Avila of Delibes's childhood did not fill the footprint of its medieval pride, and its inhabitants were like those of Nîmes, Arles and Lucca who in the Dark Ages left their houses and retreated inside the walls of Roman amphitheatres. 'I was born in Avila, the old city of the walls', explains Delibes's protagonist, 'and I believe that the silence and the near-mystical absorption of this city settled in my soul at the very moment of birth.'

But I grew up in a world of relentless progress, so why should I have fallen under that soporific spell of decay? I was born in Welwyn Garden City, whose first brick was laid in 1922. Avila is encircled by eighty-eight battlemented towers, Welwyn by the creosoted fences of housing estates,

A seventeenth century drawing of the amphitheatre at Arles. During the lawlessness of the Dark Ages, the people abandoned their houses and built homes inside the walls of the Roman amphitheatre.

by playing-fields and business parks. Hertfordshire is the county of New Towns: within a radius of 15 miles from the village in which we lived were Letchworth – the first Garden City – and Welwyn, and the post-war towns of Stevenage, Hatfield and Hemel Hempstead. It was many years before I realised the village was old, but its populace was wealthy, fit and extremely healthy, the lanes gleaming with BMWs, children's bicycles and joggers in Lycra. Our neighbours were in the City, insurance, or computing. The single speck of decay on the shiny, blue horizon was the manor house. It was the home of the Cleverdons, and Mr Cleverdon had the rustiest car in the village. When I was young I could not understand why he had a clapped-out Volvo but three boys at Eton, a house with thirty windows but holes in his sweater. The wealth of our parents – and our friends' parents – was measured in salaries and investments, in health insurance, school fees and pension funds, and was as precisely numerical as the train timetable to the City. The Cleverdons' manner of wealth was incomprehensible by contrast: wealth like a cluttered attic, a cash dividend from blowing the dust off the sideboard when the man from Christie's called.

The estate formed the boundary to the village, its mossy flint wall ignoring the disapproving glare of a new estate of bright new Lego-like houses opposite. In places the wall had tumbled, and as children we climbed inside to toboggan, climb trees, or pester the cattle. No one chased us away. Indeed, apart from the occasional sighting of the cowman, we saw no one on the lawns, or on the tennis courts, or in the greenhouses. The windows in the long, grey façade were shuttered, and the only sign of life inside was when – crawling through the rhododendrons once – we saw through the open front door the flicker of firelight on the oak panelling in the hall, and rows of stags' antlers. Trespassing in Cleverdons' I felt inexplicably at home, more at ease in one of the rotting garden pavilions than in a friend's living-room, happier to play football on their scuffed tennis court than in the public recreation ground.

I never entered the house, nor spoke to anyone. I cannot pretend to have had a dramatic, life-changing encounter there but the memory of this attraction was puzzling enough for me to return twenty years later. I soon realised that my impulse as a child was not – as I had feared at the gates, picturing the advertisement in *Country Life* – a social aspiration. I had no sense of acquisitiveness.

It was Christmas Eve, and trees in drifts of presents were displayed in the windows of every front room in the village. No festive lights twinkled at Cleverdons'. A friend had come from London with me, and at the dairy farm we broke the ice on the cattle-trough with a puerile clattering of sticks and stones. On the tennis court the lines had still not been repainted, and the net sagged with frosted mildew. We play-acted a game, chasing an imaginary ball through the dead leaves and gasping 'pop', because – I think – my friend was studying film and had just watched Antonioni's *Blow-up*.

The house remained silent. Smoke came from the chimney, but the shutters were closed; indeed, they might not have been opened in the past twenty years. As children we had counted the windows and argued over the number of rooms inside: twelve windows across, three storeys high, and an attic. Were there ten, fifteen, or twenty bedrooms? Our house had five but no cellar or stable loft, no space which was dusty, or cluttered, or secret. It was a new house and we had long since explored every inch of floor space – under beds, behind the machines in the utility room – with a child's microscopic, beetling scrutiny.

Next, returning that Christmas, I went in search of an old bridge which spanned a river valley some distance from the house. We had enacted set-pieces from the Second World War there, charging across with a rat-tat-tat from machine-guns made of tree branches. The stream was dry in the winter, and whatever road had once crossed the bridge was now buried by pasture. The brick structure was – I recognised, with the hindsight of a professional architectural historian – built in the eighteenth century as an ornamental feature, carrying visitors in their carriages on a Picturesque ride around the estate. The stone parapet was carved in the form of a Doric cornice, and pieces had tumbled into the dry gully below. The paving stones were covered by long grass, slicked flat by the frost. It was so brilliant a sky that I lay on my back on the crown of the bridge. Despite the chill, I felt an elated quietude. The silence was made audible by the distant purr of traffic on the motorway. It must have been many years since the wheels of any vehicle had trundled over this curve. Its neglect – the loose stones, the brambles growing in the cracks, the lush grass, even the dryness of the water-course – seemed to be a gentle denial of the purpose for which the bridge was built, a negation of the forward impulse of the high stone arch. In ruins movement is halted, and Time suspended. The dilapidated bridge was the still point of a spinning world which moved forward day by day. Beyond the wall of Cleverdon's estate was a world in which every day was an advance towards a richer, fitter, cleaner and perhaps happier future. Its decaying embrace was a refuge from a suburban time-clock.

It was getting dark, and in the sky I could see the glow of the lights of the motorway, of Stevenage and Welwyn Garden City. Leaving the house I now understood the physical, magnetic attraction of so many features in the countryside which have been stranded by the march of progress. Picture the gates of a country house which have been locked ever since the side entrance came into use: stone piers green with lichen, ivy climbing the rusty gilding of the ironwork, grass between the cobbles of a courtyard in which carriages once clattered to a breathless halt. Or perhaps the house is gone, and the iron gates sold for scrap, the stone piers standing alone in a trackless field. We have the equivalents of ancient aqueducts in the viaducts of disused railways, their muddy paths overhung with blackberry bushes and the arches of Victorian engineering brick as proudly and massively redundant as the Roman masonry. I pause too at petrol stations on old high roads, shut down when a by-pass opens. Rusty pumps stand to attention, peeling posters shout special offers, and on the pitted tarmac of the forecourt you can hear the traffic roaring on the dual carriageway over the hill.

In 1802 William and Dorothy Wordsworth were walking the valley of the Rye, and Dorothy left the path to explore the ruins of the twelfth-century abbey of Rievaulx. She 'went down to look at the Ruins – thrushes were singing, cattle feeding among green grown hillocks about the Ruins. . . . I could have stayed in this solemn quiet spot till evening without a thought of moving, but William was waiting for me, so in a quarter of an hour I went away.' The first attraction of architectural decay is the seductive stillness she describes. I have lost count of the number of evenings in which I have idled in remote ruins until darkness falls, and then spent a desperate evening in search of the lights of a town. Lingering inside the frescoed saloon of a sugar-planter's palace in Cuba and then rushing to pedal home through the sugar-cane before the tracks disappear into the darkness; missing the ferry back across the Bosphorus because I was unable to leave the ruins of the Byzantine castle on the hilltop with its views of the black tankers crawling silently like slugs across the surface of the Black Sea below, the only sound in this panorama of two continents the hobbled bleat of a goat. If I am lonely in a foreign country, I search for ruins. Later in that journey through Turkey I was sodden and dejected after three days of rain, but on the morning that the sky cleared discovered the temple in the deep, green valley of Euromos. In the sudden spring sunshine flowers blossomed between the fallen columns. A Turkish family stopped for lunch there, and I played football with the two teenage sons inside the chamber of the temple. The boys did not speak a word of English but the ball's unpredictable ricochet from fluted marble goal-posts was breathlessly hilarious.

In Mérida, the Roman capital of Spain, two aqueducts built by the legions span the River Guadiana. One is intact, and water still flows across. We stood and admired the engineers' design and construction of its mighty granite arches, read the guidebook for a few minutes, and then moved on. The second aqueduct collapses into ruins in the middle of the river, with storks nesting in the crumbling parapet. Without a word of discussion, my friends and I chose that spot to idle in for the afternoon. The only sound in the siesta was the frogs croaking in the reeds which clustered where the fallen stones dam the river. We only stirred when the sun moved behind the aqueduct. If I am stressed or unhappy, I close my eyes and remember these moments of absolute peace in the embrace of ruins, and castles and temples and city walls return to give me the happiness of a child, drowsy after a hectic summer's day.

The examples are innocuous, I realise. If its architectural expression in the Home Counties of England seems trivial, go to Rome and walk the Appian Way from the city walls out into the countryside. It is flanked by the tombs of noble citizens and for the first 2 or 3 miles (3 or 4 kilometres) you are excited by the intactness of the carriageway: it is easy to imagine a legion on these flagstones and pace yourself to their quick, jangling march. But as the grassy chinks between them widen, as the slabs separate and disappear into the gathering scrub, the urge to move forward diminishes. Even the proud milestones are lethargic, the chiselled numerals yawning under their veil of moss. Time is suspended, or reversed, or erased; it is hard to say which, but for Charles Dickens, in 1846, as dusk fell it was the end of the world:

> Now we tracked a piece of the old road above the ground; now we traced it underneath a grassy covering, as if that were its grave; but all the way was ruin. In the distance, ruined aqueducts went stalking on their giant course across the plain. . . . The unseen larks above us, who alone disturbed the awful silence, had their nests in ruin; and the fierce herdsmen, clad in sheepskins, who now and then scowled upon us from their sleeping nooks, were housed in ruin. . . . I almost felt as if the sun would never rise again, but look its last, that night, upon a ruined world.

I was married in Rome last summer – Anna is a Roman – and the party afterwards was on the Appian Way. The coach driver was unable to traverse the final stretch and in the dusk it was hilarious to see the English girls in high heels giggling as they tripped over the ancient flagstones. The party was in a villa on the road of tombs, one of the many farmhouses acquired by wealthy Romans after the last war and converted into plush haciendas. The citizens who live there today are as rich as those buried two thousand years ago, and on Sunday lunchtimes the roads to the countryside are jammed with new Mercedes and Alfa Romeos. In the last fifty years speculators have built grubby, concrete tower blocks for two million new residents, and in Italy these *subborghi* are the equivalent of our inner cities, where Pasolini was murdered, and where Fellini set his film *Nights of Cabiria*. Fly into Fiumicino Airport and as you drive into Rome your eye can follow the arches of the Acqua Felice aqueduct striding away into the tall flats, highways and garden centres which have replaced the mighty old walls as the boundary of the Eternal City.

Until the twentieth century the Campagna was a melancholy and desolate shore encircling the sacred island. Its villages, infested with malaria, had remained abandoned until Mussolini drained the land in the 1920s. In Caesar's time fields of yellow corn had filled the horizon but the Goths ruptured the aqueducts and the floods turned the fields to swamps. In the seventeenth and eighteenth centuries it was deserted but for shepherds and painters, and the tinctures of light on its stubbly grass, its tufty ruins and its cattle have been immortalised in the paintings of Nicolaes Berchem, Claude Lorraine and Corot. Travellers on the Grand Tour hastened their carriages towards the distant glint of the dome of St Peter's. Scrawny sheep straggled across the dreary, weed-ridden heath, with its shepherds' huts assembled from the debris of Roman ruins; how unlike the English countryside with its neat hedges and plump sheep and warm cottages. William Beckford was an exception, halting his retinue in order to meditate in the wilderness. Stooping under an antique marble frieze which formed the lintel of a shepherd's hut he traced words on the sandy floor and murmured 'a melancholy song. . . . Perhaps, the dead listened to me from their narrow cells. The living I can answer for; they were far enough removed.'

After Pauline de Beaumont's death Chateaubriand rode through the same wilderness until he reached the tomb of the Roman maiden Cecilia Metella, the circular drum which is the most imposing monument on the Appian Way. Chateaubriand offers the most disturbing single image of how Rome and the Campagna overturned the expectations of a visitor from the populous, booming north: not only did the dead outnumber the living but 'There are more tombs than dead in this city. I imagine that the deceased, when they feel too warm in their marble resting-place, glide into another that has remained empty, even as a sick man is moved from one bed to another. One seems to hear the bodies pass, during the night, from coffin to coffin.'

An early American tourist had never seen human progress reversed until he entered the 'dreary desert' of the Campagna. Visiting in 1821, Theodore Dwight described a phenomenon his countrymen could not believe existed:

> How unlike is such a scene as this, to the first view of
> one of our American cities . . . Instead of the cheerful
> and exhilarating sight of a savage wilderness retreating
> before the progress of a free and enlightened society . . .
> here we have the poor remains of that mighty city – the
> cradle and grave of an empire so long triumphant on

earth – now dwindling away before the widespread
desolation which surrounds it, and shrinking back upon
itself, as if for dread of an invisible destroyer.

No one has written better on this melancholy landscape
than the young Henry James, who on his first visit to Rome
as a young man rode out daily through the city walls in
several changing seasons. Just a few months before his
horizon had been 'the raw plank fence of a Boston suburb',
plastered with advertisements for patent medicine. Now he
was spellbound:

[An aqueduct] stands knee-deep in the flower-strewn

*The Tomb of Caecilia Metella*, by Oswald Achenbach, late 19c. This mausoleum is the most imposing on the Appian Way, and was built in the first century BC in memory of Caecilia Metella. To Romantics such as Chateaubriand, Byron and Madame de Staël, the maiden's tomb was a place to meditate on love and death.

grass, and its rugged piers are hung with ivy as the columns of a church are draped for a festa. Every archway is a picture, massively framed, of the distance beyond – of the snow-tipped Sabines and lonely Socrate. As the spring advances the whole Campagna smiles and waves with flowers; but I think they are nowhere more rank and lovely than in the shifting shadow of aqueducts, where they muffle the feet of the columns and smother the ½-dozen brooks which wander in and out like silver meshes between the legs of a file of giants. . . . [The aqueducts] seem the very source of the solitude in which they stand; they look like architectural spectres and loom through the light

mists of their grassy desert, as you recede along the line,
with the same insubstantial vastness as if they rose out
of the Egyptian sands.

Here, in the sunlight, James composes in words his version
of a painting by Claude or Corot. But as the benign light
fades the Campagna becomes its true self: a menacing,
chilling deadness. James quickened his pace homewards but
could not resist peering into the courtyards of the decrepit,
sinister farmhouses on the way. Shutters slammed at unlit
windows; in the shadows he glimpsed a mossy staircase and
a well-head hollowed out from an ancient sacrificial altar.
One farmhouse was so sinister that he suspected a suicide lay
behind its 'bolted door and barred window':

> Every wayside mark of manners, of history, every stamp
> of the past in the country about Rome, touches my
> sense to a thrill, and I may thus exaggerate the appeal of
> very common things. This is the more likely because the
> appeal seems ever to rise out of heaven knows what
> depths of ancient trouble. To delight in the aspects of
> *sentient* ruin might appear a heartless pastime and the
> pleasure, I confess, shows the note of perversity.

Pausing before the crumbling façade James seems to have
glimpsed an understanding of the 'perversity' by which we
find a pleasure in contemplating decay. Frustratingly,
however – frustratingly for us, that is – he kicks his heels and
rides away without pausing to explain. But we do realise that
the answer is as likely to be found in the front yard of an
ordinary house as in the arena of the Colosseum.

## III
# Haunted Houses

That over there is your house,
All covered over with trees and bushes.
Rabbits had run in at the dog-hole,
Pheasants flew down from the beam of the roof.
In the courtyard was growing some wild grain,
And by the wall some wild mallows.
I'll boil the grain and make porridge,
I'll pluck the mallows and make soup.
Soup and porridge are both cooked,
But there is no one to eat them with.
I went out and looked towards the east,
While tears fell and wetted my clothes.

A soldier has returned from the wars, and a villager tells him of the fate of his home. The poem was written in China in the first century BC. The poignancy of a return to a ruined home is one of the oldest and most universal themes in literature.

In Zanzibar the ruins of the palaces of the Arab sultans who ruled the island in the nineteenth century stand surrounded by spice plantations. Bet il Mtoni was the country harem of Sejid Said, where he would be greeted by women sitting in the shade beside the lily pond. The stone basins survive under the mango-trees, and so do the columns of plastered mud which supported the verandah. The most celebrated resident of Bet il Mtoni was the sultan's daughter, Princess Salme, who eloped with a German merchant. They fled to Hamburg, where he was run over by an electric tram. In 1885, after nineteen years of cold and penurious exile, Frau Ruete was permitted to come home for a few precious days. At Bet il Mtoni she collapsed with nostalgia:

> What a sight! In place of a palace there was nothing but a fast decaying ruin. . . . The baths, once such a favourite place of resort, and always filled with such a merry throng, had lost their roofs. . . . There I stood gazing with burning eyes at the neglect and desolation around with the recollection of former and happier days filling my heart with a painful mockery of all things earthly and human. . . . The figures of former residents seemed to me to be hovering around and gliding from under the dangerously-leaning roofs, the half-hanging doors and falling beams. More and more vividly did their faces and shapes grow upon me. I was moving in their midst, and could hear their own familiar voices. How long this delusion lasted I know not, but I was suddenly roused into the actual present again by my children coming to draw me away from the scenes that affected me so deeply.

Returning to the cold fireside in Hamburg she wrote her autobiography recalling her childhood in an island which had no winter, a childhood so indulged that she was woken each morning by slaves massaging spices and oils into the soles of her feet.

Osbert Lancaster's autobiography, *All Done from Memory* (1963), begins during a black-out in the Blitz: he finds himself in North Kensington, the area in which he lived as a child in the 1900s but which had since fallen into poverty. The silence of streets deserted after the air raid tempts him to explore deeper. Moonlight gleams on the crumbling cornices and porticoes of the 'vast stucco palaces' which had once been the 'Acropolis of Edwardian propriety' but were now slums. His reverie is interrupted by a house which is uniform in its dereliction but oddly familiar. Looking closely, he sees that the house must have been

> intended for some solid family of the Victorian bourgeoisie; the marked disparity of the window curtains on the various floors, all subtly different in their general cheapness and vulgarity, indicated that it now sheltered three or four perhaps separate establishments. My glance travelling disdainfully across this depressing façade, marking the broken balustrade above the cornice, the hacked and blackened lime trees, the half erased 79 on the dirty umber of the door-pillars that had once been cream, came finally and shockingly to rest on the street-name attached to the garden wall – Elgin Crescent. This, I suddenly realised, was my birthplace.

This jarring dislocation in locality and Time led Lancaster to meditate on the decline and fall of the culture of his birth: the decent but unfashionable upper middle classes. He began the autobiography to record a stratum of society whose disappearance no one seemed to regret, or even to

No. 79 Elgin Crescent, London, drawn by Osbert Lancaster as the
frontispiece to *All Done from Memory* (1963).

notice. In 1942 he was in his early middle age but many centuries seemed to separate the façade before him from a world of dancing classes on the beeswaxed floors behind the tall windows, and carriages setting down for receptions at gas-lit, shining white porches. The condition of these houses reflected the shiftless, fractured modern world, their varying shades of cheap curtains indicating 'Viennese professors and Indian students and bed-sitter business girls'. The Edwardian Acropolis was a ruin which sheltered 'refugees from every part of the once civilised world, like the dark-age troglodytes who sheltered in the galleries and boxes of the Coliseum'.

In fiction, the subtlest version of the theme of the return to the ruined house is John Cheever's short story 'The Swimmer', set in the prosperous suburbs of New York. The ten-page story is a miniature masterpiece, expanded into a haunting film starring Burt Lancaster. Its protagonist Ned Merrill is the embodiment of the aspirations of the upper middle classes in 1960s America, and the story begins as he drinks highballs beside the Westerhazys' pool one Sunday lunchtime in midsummer. 'Why, it's Ned! How great to see you! How's Lucinda? How's those pretty girls? Still running that little red Jaguar? Why don't you ever reply to our invitations? Stay for lunch.' Told that the Howletts have put in a pool, he realises that there is now a swimming pool in every garden until his own 8 miles away. With the sudden vision of a necklace of jewel-blue pools glinting through the haze of the wooded valley he decides to swim home. Ned is a hero when he plunges into the Westerhazys' pool – 'Ned, you're still fitter than any of us!' – and as he strides away across the lawn in blue swimming trunks he projects a weight of success in the carriage of his college athlete shoulders alone. At each pool in the sequence an illusion falls away. Through the sideways glances of Ned's neighbours we learn that Lucinda has left, the girls are tearaways, and Ned a bankrupt. At the Welchers' the pool is empty, the deckchairs stacked away, and the bath-house locked. At the front of the house he finds a FOR SALE sign. But had not he and Lucinda had dinner there last week? 'Was his memory failing or had he so disciplined it in the repression of unpleasant facts that he had damaged his sense of the truth?'

As he limps up the drive of his own house his shoulders are slumped, and his body shivers with the chill of the fading afternoon. Exhausted, he can hardly push open the garden gate. His hands are stained red, he notices: the red is rust from its fancy iron bars. The shock of this realisation wakes Ned from his delusion. The lawn is overgrown, rain is puddled in the pitted asphalt of the tennis court, and – for it is suddenly and inexplicably autumn – leaves are rotting on the gravel drive. This is reality. Through the cracked window-panes of the darkened house he sees that the lounge is empty of furniture, its cocktail bar bare. The front door is padlocked, and we leave Ned crouching in the porch in his swimming trunks, at the mercy of the stormy night.

Soon there will be children pushing open the gate and tip-toeing up to the windows, whispering about the terrible fate of the Mr Merrill who once lived here. The house has become one we can all recognise: frightening because of the very familiarity of the features which have fallen into decay. As children we expect gates to lock, lawns to be mown, porch lights to shine, floors to be polished and windows to be clean and unbroken. The Merrill house has become Boo Radley's home in Harper Lee's *To Kill a Mockingbird*, its rotten porch creaking under the madman's shadow, and its rickety fence protecting a garden unkempt with 'johnson-grass and rabbit-tobacco'.

And it is Miss Havisham's house. In *Great Expectations* Pip stands at the rusty gate on the day which will change his life. The house was 'of old brick, and dismal, and had a great many iron bars to it. . . . Some of the windows had been walled up; of those that remained, all the lower were rustily barred. . . . The cold wind seemed to blow colder there, than outside the gate.' It is best pictured in David Lean's 1948 film. Dickens's original model is a handsome Georgian house which still stands off the High Street in Rochester, and it was there that the comedian Rod Hull spent the fortune he had earned from his Emu act on re-creating the sets from Lean's film.

It is Estella who opens the gate to Pip, but Satis is no sleeping beauty's palace entwined in ivy. Snow does not melt in the courtyard, and the garden is 'a rank ruin of cabbage stalks, and one box tree'. Fires sputter in the grates, and smoke hangs in the room like the mist on the river estuary. The story of Miss Havisham's betrayal by her fiancé many years before is narrated by objects which are broken or rotted: the clocks stopped at twenty to nine, the single slipper of yellowed silk, the wedding cake crawling with spiders. And her adopted daughter Estella is as sterile as Satis; she has no heart, she assures Pip, no emotional pulse.

After leaving for London to become a gentleman Pip returns to Satis frequently. What his story shows is that you can never step into the same ruin twice. Once he finds that

Estella has blossomed into a beautiful woman, and as they walk 'in the ruined garden . . . it was all in bloom for me. If the green and yellow growth of weed in the chinks of the old wall had been the most precious flowers that ever blew, it would not have been more cherished in my remembrance.' Next, he sees in Satis his own destruction. Told that the anonymous benefactor who had paid to groom the blacksmith's boy into a gentleman is not Miss Havisham but the convict Magwitch, Pip realises that he has turned his back on honest Joe's forge to pursue a selfish fantasy of himself. At his next visit he listens to Estella recite a list of suitors she has withered with her cold eye and he understands too that she was bred to be Miss Havisham's instrument of revenge on the male sex. Staring at her stooped and wicked silhouette projected by firelight on to the wall, Pip perceives his own degradation:

> My thoughts passed into the great room across the
> landing where the table was spread, and I saw it written,
> as it were, in the falls of the cobwebs from the
> centrepiece, in the crawlings of the spiders on the cloth,
> in the tracks of the mice as they betook their little
> quickened hearts behind the panels, and in the gropings
> and pausings of the beetles on the floor.

By the time of his final visit to Satis he is a redeemed man. For eleven years he has worked as a clerk in the colonies, having sacrificed his own expectations in order to rescue his friends. Satis has been demolished, and hoardings advertise that new houses will be built on the site. In the misty twilight which closes the novel, Pip walks over the foundations and reconstructs the hallways and corridors in his memory. He is interrupted by the arrival of Estella on the scene. She has returned too, now that her well-bred brute of a husband has died; he squandered her fortune, but she sold the house last of all. But Estella has learned what it is to have a vulnerable heart, and she and Pip leave as friends. Life begins anew in the destruction. 'Some of the old ivy had struck root anew, and was growing green in the low quiet mounds of ruin.'

In Dickens architecture is the material expression of the human spirit, so that Miss Havisham's sadness and sterility solidify into brick and stone. In Edgar Allan Poe's story *The Fall of the House of Usher* the analogy between the building and its occupants is made even more explicit. Castle and family are synonymous to the local peasantry, but the stones are more alive than the people, the narrator discovers. He has come to stay with his old schoolfriend Roderick Usher, riding across a landscape whose few trees have been bleached by decay. Beside a lake whose waters are as black and stagnant as tar, and exhaling a leaden-hued mist, stands the ancient Gothic castle. From the causeway its structure appears intact, but on closer inspection has 'the specious totality of old woodwork which has rotted for long years in some neglected vault, with no disturbance from the breath of external air'. Its stones are covered with a rootless fungus, as if the condensation of the air's active malevolence.

Roderick Usher has not stepped outside for many years, and has been slowly poisoned by the atmosphere of his ancestral home: 'an effect which the *physique* of the grey walls and turrets, and of the dim tarn into which they all looked down, had, at length, brought about upon the *morale* of his existence'. For centuries the spirit of the castle 'had moulded the destinies of his family, and . . . made him what I now saw him – what he was'. He is impotent, neurotic and cadaverous, agitated at the sounds from the castle vaults far below. Roderick has buried his sister Madeline in their depths but she has risen from a catatonic trance, and the noise of her fingernails scraping on the iron seal of the tomb penetrates through stone walls as if through shredded paper. The din in his inflamed ear grows louder and louder, until his grimy, white-faced sister bursts into the room and the two last Ushers expire in a fatal embrace.

As the narrator flees across the causeway, there is a sudden radiance in the black water. It is the reflection of a blood-red moon shining through a crack in the castle wall, a crack which widens until the structure splits in two, 'and the deep and dark tarn at my feet closed sullenly and silently over the fragments of the HOUSE OF USHER'.

Poe's analogy of the castle with the Usher family was so explicit that in noting how the doors and windows in the façade represent Roderick's mouth and eyes A. E. Housman observed, tartly, that hopefully the 'winged odours' rising like mist from the tufty castle brow 'have no connection with hair oil'. At a deeper level, however, Poe explained that he intended 'to imply a mind haunted by phantoms, a disordered brain'. Writing in 1923, D. H. Lawrence recognised that the subterranean neurosis in *Usher* made Poe 'an adventurer into the vaults and cellars and horrible underground passages of the human soul'. In his view, Poe's exposure of 'the disintegration process of his own psyche' prefigured the neurosis of twentieth-century humankind. Poe prefigured Freud, who saw archaeology as an analogy for the practice of psychoanalysis. 'Stones speak', said Freud, and every fragment must be uncovered, studied and analysed as a piece of evidence in a larger meaning. On Wilhelm Jensen's novel of 1903, *Gradiva*, a romance set in Pompeii, Freud wrote: 'What had formerly been the city of Pompeii assumed an entirely changed appearance, but not a living one; it now appeared rather to become petrified in dead immobility. Yet out of it stirred a feeling that death was beginning to talk.'

In his depiction of subterranean neuroses Poe was a prophet of modernity but – ragged, stained and rancorous, reeking of drink and rejection – not a prophet respectable people feel comfortable to stand beside. Poe's *Fall of the House of Usher* is the extreme expression of the literary Gothic which had begun with Horace Walpole's *Castle of Otranto* a century before, and it was writers who demonstrated to architects that the cellars, towers and shadows of medieval ruins touched recesses in the soul which were unmoved by the classical. Despite this literature, and its illustrations, the vividness of Poe's architectural depictions remains something of a puzzle. He and his foster parents arrived in London in 1815, when he was six, and stayed until he was ten. During this time they travelled to Scotland, and into Devon and Gloucestershire. No one knows which abbeys or castles they visited but it is tempting to speculate.

Such ruins are potent to children, and it was in the ruins of a medieval abbey that the last Lord Byron enjoyed a childhood that might have been imagined by Poe. Newstead Abbey, near Nottingham, is England's House of Usher. At Christmas time in 1811 a young man named William

Harness rode beside a vast and stagnant lake towards the house, to renew a friendship with Byron begun at Harrow ten years before. 'It was winter,' he recalled, 'dark, dreary weather – the snow upon the ground; and a straggling, gloomy, depressive, partially-inhabited place the Abbey was.' London was full of rumours of Byron's orgies, and Harness was perhaps a little disappointed to report that 'nothing could be more quiet and regular than the course of our days'.

The thirteenth-century abbey had been acquired by Sir John Byron during Henry VIII's dissolution of the monasteries, and converted into a house. All that remained of the monks' church was the gaunt silhouette of the entrance façade, a 'yawning arch' with broken tracery like splintered teeth. The poet was the sixth and last Lord Byron. The fifth lord, the 'wicked Lord Byron', had bankrupted the estate by his whims, which included the construction of 'folly' castles on the lakes and bombarding them with a toy navy crewed by boys from the estate. According to the local legend, he lived his final years in the only dry room in the abbey, the kitchen, alone but for a serving girl and his tame crickets. The moment he expired the crickets marched out of the house. The fifth lord's body lay mouldering for a month because there was not enough money to pay an undertaker.

It was only the sudden death of a cousin serving in the navy which, unexpectedly, made Byron heir to his great-uncle's estate. Ten years old, a robust but club-footed boy, he was living with his mother in a furnished flat in Aberdeen, his dissolute father – 'Mad Jack' Byron – having abandoned them to die in Paris. It was some months before they could afford the coach-fare south. But Newstead, although vast, was not the mansion they had imagined. The oaks lining the 2-mile drive had been felled to pay the grocer's bill and inside the house bales of hay were stashed in the halls and cattle stabled in the corridors. The chill forced the Byrons to rent the abbey to a tenant farmer and move to a flat in London. When he was at school at Harrow he would spend holidays in the lodges to the estate, now let to Lord Grey de Ruthyn. The two noblemen were enthusiastic shots and became inseparable friends, ignoring the estate manager's grumbles that they were letting the land become a wilderness in order to provide better cover for hares and pheasants. But in the spring of 1804 – when Byron was still only fifteen – he was molested by Grey and fled Newstead.

The sixth Lord Byron inherited the mouldering ruin of Newstead Abbey, a thirteenth-century Priory near Mansfield, when he was ten years old.

Byron did not live in the abbey until he was twenty-one, by which time he was an undergraduate of prodigious charisma and talent at Trinity College, Cambridge. But we cannot understand the melancholia and introspection – or the egotism and snobbery – which were inseparable from his creativity as a poet without understanding these years at Newstead. He was a lonely boy who hobbled through the wild woods or swam with a favourite dog in the sludgy lakes, exploring the ruined cloisters and dreaming of the monks buried there and of the exploits of his notorious Byron ancestors. But he was living in the lodge while a tenant's fire blazed in the abbey hearth. Pride in that inheritance was inseparable from a consciousness of his family's decay and the fear that – in his own words – he was 'the wreck of the line'. At eighteen he wrote:

> Newstead! What saddening change of scene is thine!
> Thy yawning arch betokens slow decay;
> The last and youngest of a noble line,
> Now holds thy mouldering turrets in his sway.

When Grey's lease expired Byron was heavily in debt, and he returned with the intention of selling Newstead. He fell in love with the house, however, and redecorated a suite of rooms with plush upholstery and furniture. Five years later rain would be pouring through the ceilings but Byron had neither the funds nor the inclination to repair the basic structure of the building. His only architectural commissions were a monument to his dog Boatswain placed on the site of the high altar of the abbey church, and a plunge-pool installed in the cloister. This 'dark, and cold, cellar-like hole, must have required good courage to plunge into', wrote Nathaniel Hawthorne when he made a pilgrimage to the abbey. It is a dreary little cellar now, but when the keeper unlocks the oak Tudor door the gloom still reverberates with Byron's boisterous laughter.

In the summer of 1809 his friends from Cambridge came to stay, joining the wolf and the bear already quartered in the abbey to play at being 'the merry monks of Newstead'. Breakfast was never before noon, recalled Charles Skinner Matthews, and the afternoon was occupied by 'reading, fencing, single-stick, or shuttle-cock in the great-room – practising with pistols in the hall – walking, riding, cricket – sailing on the lake – playing with the bear or teasing the wolf. Between seven and eight we dined, and our evening lasted from that time till one, two, or three in the morning.' At dinner they dressed in habits hired from a theatrical costumier and took turns to drink claret from a monk's skull, 'From which, unlike a living head / Whatever flows is never dull'. The skull had been dug up in the garden and polished into a cup set on a silver base by a jeweller in Nottingham.

> Monastic dome! Condemned to uses vile!
> Where superstition once had made her den
> Now Paphian girls were known to sing and smile.

The protagonist in Byron's *Childe Harold* inherits an ancient abbey and these opening lines added credence to the rumours about the events of that summer. The reality was more straightforward: there were no orgies, just draughty chambers noisy with shuttlecock, pistol-shots, yapping animals and friendly laughter.

Two summers later Byron returned from the balls of London in order to bury his mother. He could not bring himself to follow the funeral cortège but stopped in the doorway. When her coffin had disappeared from sight, he summoned a servant into the hall for a boxing match: all his life he was to combat depression with furious physical activity, as when he swam far out to sea during Shelley's funeral on the beach in the Bay of Spezia. A few days after his mother's death the mischievous and brilliant Matthews was tragically drowned in the River Cam. The autumn brought news of a third sudden death: Christopher Edleston, the choirboy with whom he had been besotted as an undergraduate. Newstead would never be the same as in that hilarious summer of 1809. The aspect of the ruin changed:

> In the Dome of my Sires as the clear moonbeam falls
> Through Silence and Shade o'er its desolate walls . . .

> And the step that o'er-echoes the gray floor of stone
> Falls suddenly now, for 'tis only my own.

Many years later a friend asked how Byron could bear to remain in Venice during its depressing winter. 'I have been familiar with ruins too long to dislike desolation,' the poet replied. By this time Byron had left England for good, having sold Newstead in 1816. He had clung to this ancestral legacy until huge debts made its sale inevitable.

Byron had encountered his first classical ruins on a journey through Europe to Greece and Istanbul in 1808 with John Cam Hobhouse. He was more interested in Nature than in marble jigsaws, however, and while Hobhouse studied epitaphs he ascended to the heights of Parnassus:

> They had haunted my dreams from boyhood; the pines, eagles, vultures and owls were descended from those Themistocles and Alexander had seen, and were not degenerated like the humans; the rocks and torrents the same. John Cam's dogged persistence in pursuit of his hobby is to be envied; I have no hobby and no perseverance. I gazed at the stars and ruminated; took no notes, asked no questions.

At Ephesus Hobhouse continued his research but as Byron stood in the ruins between the steep green hillsides and the sea, he was alert to a deeper resonance than epitaphs could tell. He absorbed the sadness of the 'dramatic barking of jackals . . . a mixed and mournful sound which bayed from afar complainingly'. He was sensitive to a profound spiritual desolation.

On his return to London the publication of *Childe Harold* made Byron a celebrity and it is here that we somehow lose sight of the boisterous and vulnerable boy, whirled away by the adulation of society. In his final years he is an elusive figure, distanced by irony, lust and flattery, and so jaded that when in Venice he was caught climbing a young girl's balcony he did not care, he said, if her father had him shot, or married.

To understand Byron we must always return to

Newstead. 'If I am a poet the air of Greece has made me one,' he is reported to have said. No. It was not the warm south which made Byron a poet but the clammy mists of a ruined English abbey. His genius germinated in the damp shadows of ancient decay.

## IV

# Ephesus without an Umbrella

Thanks to the rain I was the only tourist in the ruins of Ephesus, sheltering under a canopy of fig leaves. It was March and the vegetation had not yet been trimmed that year. In the amphitheatre where St Paul once preached shafts of fennel shot up higher than a man's head and away from the tourist paths the grass was waist high, with the tumbled columns as slippery as logs underfoot.

The Greek colony of Ephesus died over many centuries, slowly strangled by the River Meander's change of course: the river wriggled away, and the harbour filled with silt. The road to the sea disappears into marshland now but it is still possible to imagine the way lit with lamps, and the Ephesians strolling down to the quay to watch the sailors unloading their triremes and to hear news from distant shores. Night fell on my visit, and when the rain slackened a shepherd led his goats across the steep hillside. Their bells echoed in the darkening ruins. Eventually two soldiers on guard discovered me, and as we stepped over the puddles on the marble pavement they were polite enough to share an umbrella. In my hotel later that evening I noticed a poster which showed the Sacred Way in the tourist season, as crowded with brightly clothed figures as a shopping mall, and with no vegetation to soften the glare of marble.

'Turkey: An Open Air Museum' read the caption. But, no: a ruin is not an open air museum.

Byron's friend Percy Bysshe Shelley placed ruins at the centre of his personal and political philosophy. When he and his family passed through Rome in the autumn of 1818 the greatest surprise was the abundance of Nature within the city walls. They returned to live in Rome the following spring, and each morning he made the brisk twenty-minute walk from lodgings in the Via del Corso through the Forum and Circus Maximus, past fields of flowers and vineyards and grassy mounds of ancient pottery, to the Baths of Caracalla. His pockets were stuffed with pens, ink-horn and a small notebook bound in black leather. For Shelley scribbling in the open air was no affectation and the notebook, now in the Bodleian Library, contains drafts of the greatest passages in *Prometheus Unbound*. As he wrote in the preface:

> This Poem was chiefly written upon the mountainous
> ruins of the Baths of Caracalla, among the flowery
> glades, and the thickets of odiferous blossoming trees,
> which are extended in ever winding labyrinths upon its
> immense platforms and dizzy arches suspended in the
> air. The bright blue sky of Rome, and the effect of the
> vigorous awakening spring in that divinest climate, and
> the new life with which it drenches the spirits even to
> intoxication, were the inspiration of this drama.

The Baths were begun by Emperor Caracalla in AD 217 and were the most magnificent in ancient Rome. Fifteen hundred bathers congregated in a sequence of vaulted halls spaced around a swimming pool. It is hard to describe the magnitude of these arches. The central pool was the model for the main concourse of Pennsylvania Station in New York and when John Dyer, author of *The Ruins of Rome*, visited in 1724 he told his brother that 'Its rooms seem to have been vastly large, and noble in comparison to the trees which have shot up within them, which, though pretty large, appear but tufts'. The walls were clad with shimmering marble – now stripped away to expose the brick – and decorated with statues as great as the Farnese Hercules. The torso of Hercules was found in the Baths of Caracalla, the head at the bottom of a well in the Trastevere, and his legs in a village 10 miles (16 kilometres) south of Rome. The Baths fell into decay when the aqueducts were ruptured in the sixth century AD and, standing some distance from the centre, they remained isolated in the wilderness in Shelley's time.

Richard Holmes considers *Prometheus Unbound* to be one of the writer's four masterpieces, and his exegesis in the biography *Shelley: The Pursuit* is the finest evocation of the fusion between ruins and a writer's imagination. 'So let man be free' is the motto of the drama. Shelley inverted the story as told by Aeschylus, so that Jove becomes a cruel tyrant and Prometheus the hero who gives to mankind liberty and love, the power of speech, science, cities and music. He is chained to the rock by Jove, under whose tyrannical rule man and Nature wither with disease and poverty. When Prometheus is released, Earth is revived. Hope is achieved through suffering.

When he arrived in Rome that spring Shelley himself was suffering, depressed by the condition of Europe and by mishaps in his own life. In his native country this was the year of the Peterloo massacre, and he had been shunned by society and rejected by his family for his atheism, his radical politics and his elopements. With Mary Godwin and her half-sister Claire Claremont he travelled through France, and saw a country exhausted by the long wars and a monarch restored to the throne. In Italy the people had been reduced to a despicable poverty by centuries of superstition and tyranny. The Venetian Republic had been annexed by the Hapsburgs after Waterloo. Rome was ruled by a Pope. And if he continued south? The Bourbon kingdoms of Naples and Sicily. East? The empire of the Ottoman despots. There was nowhere to go. All Europe was fettered by tyranny.

It was in the ruins of ancient Rome that Shelley found hope for the future – more specifically, in the flowers and trees which blossomed in the Baths of Caracalla. Its mighty walls represented the power of tyranny: the power of Caracalla, of the Bourbons, the Hapsburgs and the 'old, mad, blind, despised and dying' King George III of England. But the structure erected by the cruellest of emperors was crumbling, as the roots of figs and myrtles and laurel loosened the masonry. Their exuberant and wild fecundity promised the inevitable victory of Nature – a Nature which was fertile, democratic and free.

The discovery had the rapture of an epiphany, and in the ruins that spring Shelley regained the guiding trajectory of his short, fiery life. Nature had never seemed more beautiful than in its destruction of tyranny, as when the release of Prometheus restores the purity of Earth's spirit:

Which breath now rises, as amongst tall weeds
A violet's exhalation, and it fills
With a serener light and crimson air
Intense, yet soft, the rocks and woods around;
It feeds the quick growth of the serpent vine,
And the dark linked ivy tangling wild,
And budding, blown, or odour-faded blooms
Which star the winds with points of coloured light,
As they rain through them, and bright golden globes
Of fruit, suspended in their own green heaven . . .

The paradise of Shelley's vision is distilled from the raw experience described in a letter to his friend Thomas Love Peacock:

Never was any desolation more sublime and lovely. The perpendicular wall of ruin is cloven into steep ravines filled with flowering shrubs whose thick twisted roots are knotted in the rifts of the stones . . . the thick entangled wilderness of myrtle & bay & the flowering laurustinus . . . & the wild fig & a thousand nameless plants sown by the wandering winds [forming a] landscape like mountain hills intersected by paths like sheep tracks.

The ruins had become a work of Nature, not man, and he was reminded of the summer at Marlow two years before, when with their friend Hogg they had scrambled up the chalky, wooded bluffs above the Thames:

> The perpendicular walls resemble nothing more than
> that cliff in Bisham wood which is overgrown with
> wood, & yet is stony and precipitous – you know the
> one I mean, – not the chalk pit, but the spot which has
> that pretty copse of fir trees & privet bushes at its base,
> & where Hogg & I scrambled up & you – to my
> infinite discontent – would go home.

Read that fond, boyish letter before you visit the Baths of
Caracalla and I defy you not to be saddened – and then
angered – by the bathos of the scene now. 'Until 1870, the
Baths were one of the most beautiful spots in the world',
wrote Augustus Hare, but 'now scarcely more attractive
than the ruins of a London warehouse.' Passing through a
steel perimeter fence tourists walk on tarmac paths between
metal barriers, and underneath the arches scaffolding and
trenches and desultory labourers in hard hats give the ruins
the air of a modern construction site. The path terminates in
a grille and a DO NOT ENTER sign. Beyond is the bathers'
dressing-room, where Shelley saw the red Roman mud
dissolving to reveal a mosaic of waves in abstract patterns.
The mosaic is being conserved – hence the grille – but
however vigorously it is scrubbed the blue-black tesserae
will never shine with such brightness again.

Beside me an American family is listening to a guide's
recital of dates, measurements and social history. They are
interested, and dutiful, but do they have an inkling of the
excitement possible when this bare brick chamber was a
tumbling, scented jungle? Frustrated, I wander away from
the path to sit on a piece of marble and face the sunshine.
A guard blows his whistle, and alerts an archaeologist who

is supervising the removal of an impertinent young fig-tree from the perimeter wall. Judging by their expressions, the stubbly grass under my feet is as precious as a painted fresco. With a limp shrug I return to the prescribed path. Really, I want to tell them about Shelley, about Bisham Wood and the 'paradise of vaulted bowers / Lit by downward gazing flowers'. I want to tell them that a ruin has two values. It has an objective value as an assemblage of brick and stone, and it has a subjective value as an inspiration to artists. You can uproot that alder tree, *superintendente*, erect more fences, spray more weed-killer, excavate and polish. You will preserve every single brick for posterity, and analyse the very occasional discovery of a more ornamental fragment in a learned publication. You will have a great many bricks, but nothing more. If the archaeologists had arrived before Shelley there would be no *Prometheus Unbound*.

Archaeologists will argue that flowers and ivy on a ruin are just Picturesque fluff, curlicues to amuse an artist's pencil. What Shelley's experience shows is that the vegetation which grows on ruins appeals to the depths of our consciousness, for it represents the hand of Time, and the contest between the individual and the universe.

The next spring, in 1820, Shelley's son William died of fever in Rome. Shelley had lost children in infancy before but William had reached the age of two and his loss was by far the hardest. The Protestant cemetery was exiled to the city walls, at the point where they are overshadowed by the only pyramid in Rome, built in marble in the first century AD as the mausoleum of a citizen named Caius Cestius. A pyramid is the most imperishable form in architecture, a symbolic claim to personal immortality. In Shelley's personal philosophy, by contrast, immortality was an invisible process achieved through dissolution into a universal spirit followed by regeneration through Nature. But it was difficult to reconcile the concept with the palpable vacuum left by his plump, laughing little William. He was unable to finish the poem *In memoriam*.

> My lost William, thou in whom
> Some bright spirit lived, and did
> That decaying robe consume
> Which its lustre faintly hid,
> Here its ashes find a tomb,
> But beneath this pyramid
> Thou art not – if a thing divine
> Like thee can die, thy funeral shrine
> Is thy mother's grief and mine.
>
> Where art thou, my gentle child?
> Let me think thy spirit feeds,
> With its life intense and mild,
> The love of living leaves and weeds,
> Among these tombs and ruins wild; –
> Let me think that through low seeds
> Of the sweet flowers and sunny grass,
> Into their hues and scents may pass,
> A portion –

The pyramid of Caius Cestius stands as arrogantly impervious to Time as ever. Except that flowers uncurl between the joints in the marble blocks, delicate tentative flowers which cannot but remind us of little William. 'Who, then, was Cestius? And what is he to me?' wrote Thomas Hardy when he came to the cemetery to pay homage to the two great English poets buried there.

John Keats is commemorated by a fancy but impersonal monument, erected many years after his death in Rome in 1821 by a committee of his sentimental Victorian admirers. His friend Shelley, who died by drowning a year later, lies on the highest terrace, abutting the Roman battlements. Climbing, we pass memorials to thousands of men and women from the Protestant north and the New World. There is no greater testament to the lure of Rome than the names of these unknown pilgrims and their distant, mundane places of birth: Walmer and Hastings, Winchester and Shropshire; Wisconsin and Boston; Oslo, Copenhagen, Magdeburg, Gothenburg. Mr Bowles, late of Paddington, London, has a mighty column and a lectern-thumping epitaph. A traumatised angel flutters over the Klein daughters from New York; a cherub's tears fall on the palette of a painter of unfulfilled genius from Hamburg. Shelley's tomb is an undecorated slab, and all the more moving for its silence. If a tomb is too demonstrative – an angel obstructing our path, a hysterical maiden imploring our tears – it is a natural reaction to make one's excuses and hurry past. It is the passivity of Shelley's monument which invites the imagination: its plain, marble surface at our feet is like still shining water reflecting clouds and sunlight. It is a mirror in which Shelley's image appears, in whatever form each of us imagines him.

The poet is better here than in the morgue which the Baths of Caracalla have become. This is the most beautiful cemetery on earth; I hope there is still a plot available. It is lush and green and drowsy, the trees whirr with birds' wings, and the grass crawls with insects. The promise of continuance is not in the angels or cherubs or the stiff crosses but in this fecundity of Nature, in the ivy which effaces the chiselled letters of a name. Indeed, do we ever linger in cemeteries which are bare of vegetation? As Gustave Flaubert remarked in a letter to a friend in 1846, when he was twenty-five years old:

> Yesterday . . . I saw some ruins, beloved ruins of my youth which I knew already . . . I thought again about them, and about the dead whom I had never known and on whom my feet trampled. I love above all the sight of vegetation resting upon old ruins; this embrace of nature, coming swiftly to bury the work of man the moment his hand is no longer there to defend it, fills me with deep and ample joy.

Sailing down the River Nile four years later Flaubert observed the contest between monuments and Time played out in a brutal, desperate fight to the death. Like northern Europeans in Rome, his reaction to the ruins of the Pharaohs was based upon their contrast with the modern squalor in their shadow. Letters home to his childhood friend Louis Bouilhet concentrate on whores and catamites, but the pungent, obscene correspondence is redeemed by one startling *aperçu* when Flaubert's boat sailed into Thebes at nine o'clock in the evening, and the monuments shone a bright, stunning white in the moonlight:

The enormous white ruins looked like a troop of ghosts.
. . . I spent a night at the foot of the Colossus of
Memnon, devoured by mosquitoes. The old rascal has a
fine phizog, he's covered in graffiti. Graffiti and bird-
shit, these are the only two things on the ruins of Egypt
that indicate life. Not one blade of grass on even the
most eroded stones. They crumble to powder, like a
mummy, and that is all. The graffiti left by travellers and
the droppings of the birds of prey are the only two
ornaments of decay. You often see a great tall obelisk
with a long white stain all the way down it like a curtain,
wider at the top and narrowing towards the base. It's
the vultures, they've been coming there for centuries to
shit. The effect is very striking, and *curiously symbolic.*
Nature said to the monuments of Egypt: you want
nothing to do with me? Not even lichen will grow upon
you? All right then, damn it, I shall shit all over you.

The sterile ruins on the Nile suggested no reconciliation
between the opposing forces, unlike the lichenous ruins of
Flaubert's youth or Shelley's Baths of Caracalla. No ruin can
be suggestive to the visitor's imagination, I believe, unless
its dialogue with the forces of Nature is visibly alive and
dynamic. The suggestion is not necessarily an optimistic
one, however, and Nature's agent does not have to be
flowers or fig-trees. In the case of Van Gogh, it was the
miserable mud of Flanders.

His painting of *The Church Tower at Nuenen* (1885),
popularly called *The Peasants' Churchyard*, shows a ruined
tower surrounded by the wooden crosses which mark the
graves of the villagers. This was the period early in his career

when Van Gogh studied the rural poor – most famously in *The Potato Eaters* – and he perceived their lives and deaths as rhythms in Nature that were inevitable as the seasons of planting and harvesting. The miserable but honest crosses seem to be rooted into the squelchy earth; it is the same soil in the churchyard as in the fields. By contrast, the stone tower of the derelict church is presented as an unnatural imposition, and – by implication – religion as an alien institution which is ephemeral in comparison to the deeper cycles of Nature. This canvas, as muddy as a potato, records a profound change in Van Gogh's spirit: his loss of faith in Christianity.

In the futuristic novel *After London* (1885) Richard Jefferies used Nature as his instrument of revenge on a city he hated. Jefferies was a farmer's son from Wiltshire, a sickly mystic who became the finest nature writer of the late nineteenth century. In order to earn a living by writing for magazines he was forced to live in suburban London, in a grimy, soot-stained terrace beside the railway lines in Surbiton. He fell ill, as if poisoned. 'Putrid black water', he jotted in his diary the year before his novel was published. 'Children miserable, tortured, just the same [as in the Middle Ages]. The 21 parishes of the Lower Thames Sewage Scheme without any drainage at all. The whole place prepared for disease and pestilence . . . This W. C. century.'

His first instrument of revenge on industrial civilisation was snow. In the unfinished story 'The Great Snow' he described London slowly suffocated by an exceptional snowfall, until polar bears played on the frozen Thames and the dome of St Paul's nestled in snow-drifts. Maddened by hunger, 'The East rose and threw itself en masse upon the

West. . . . The possession of a single potato was incitement to murder.' Cannibalism followed, furniture burned and a fanatical preacher thundered:

> Where now is your mighty city that defied Nature and
> despised the conquered elements – where now is your
> pride when so simple and contemptible an agent as a
> few flakes of snow can utterly destroy it? Where are your
> steam-engines, your telegraphs and your printing-
> presses – all powerless and against what – only a little
> snow!

In the later novel the cause of destruction is not snow but a natural catastrophe, but its motivating spirit is still Jefferies's disgust in urban civilisation. *After London* is a countryman's warning to a complacent, corrupt and physically poisonous metropolis. The Thames floods and the city's blocked sewers burst to create an uninhabitable, poisonous marsh 20 miles wide and 40 miles long. The houses fall: 'For this marvellous city . . . was after all only of brick, and when the ivy grew over and trees and shrubs sprang up, and, lastly, the waters underneath burst in, this huge metropolis was soon overthrown.' The pollution of centuries condenses in a miasma which is fatal to all forms of life. 'There are no fishes, neither can eels exist in the mud, nor even newts. It is dead.' The hero Felix discovers that the ruins of the houses have crystallised to a white powder, and crumble at the touch. Skeletons lie in a blackened sand formed by millions of decomposing bodies, clutching treasure and coins. These are the treasure-hunters who have fallen victim to the miasma, and as Felix stumbles towards safety he begins to see in hallucinations the half-buried brazen statues of giants.

After the catastrophe the rich fled the country, and the survivors relapsed into a medieval barbarism. Outside London the symbolic ruins are those of the railways, for Jefferies was born near the railway town of Swindon. Rails and engines have been melted down, though 'Mounds of earth are said to still exist in the woods, which originally formed the roads for these machines, but they are now so low and covered with thickets':

> Great holes were made through the very hills for the
> passage of the iron chariot, but they are now blocked by
> the falling roofs, nor dare anyone explore such parts as
> may be open. Where are the wonderful structures with
> which the men of those days were lifted to the skies,
> rising above the clouds? These marvellous things are to
> us little more than the fables of the giants and of the old
> gods that walked upon the earth, which were fables
> even to those we call the ancients.

The few humans who remain alive cannot withstand the fecundity of Nature. Rats eat the food stores, dogs run wild, and the weeds at the edges of the fields advance to strangle the young corn. Roads disappear under brambles, yellow charlock and wild flowers, and villages are buried by silt and reeds. Through the eyes of a writer who made his reputation with telescopic descriptions of flora and fauna, we see the virulent, wild power of Nature which lies below the peaceful, trim surface of the English countryside.

The most potent demonstration of how a resurgent but

benign Nature can overcome death is the Italian city of Ninfa, destroyed and abandoned six centuries ago. An hour's drive south of Rome, it is the loveliest lost city in Europe. 'Ninfa' means nymph, and many still believe that a nymph flits through the thickets of trees which grow in the ruins. In the classical world any spring of exceptional clarity was believed to be the dwelling of an elusive, watery spirit, and Pliny's *Natural History* describes how virgin priestesses were appointed to monitor the purity of the source. The water rises today, bubbling over a gravelly bed and between bridges and fortified walls to encircle the city like a moat. A single battlemented tower is a reminder of its medieval pride; there were ten towers and fourteen churches in the thirteenth century when Pietro Caetani purchased the estate. Ninfa was valuable enough to be sacked by Barbarossa, and to see Pope Alexander III crowned there.

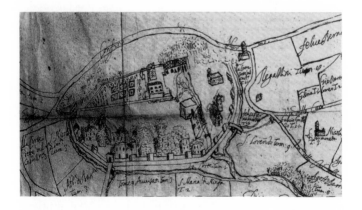

Ninfa. A medieval map showing the old town surrounded by its walls, with the rivers and springs.

During the civil wars of the late fourteenth century – in 1382, to be precise – Ninfa was destroyed. Its natural spring may have been its undoing: according to one theory, the neighbouring towns were envious of the plenitude of water and were determined to see Ninfa razed to the ground. Its houses were plundered and burned, and many of its citizens put to the sword. The rich survivors fled, and the poor followed when malaria filtered into the ruins from the encroaching marshes.

Ninfa became a lost city. In the air humid with malaria the vegetation grew with a feverish vigour, as if exhilarating in the absence of human life. The ruins became a jungle, and as a jungle it was discovered by Romantic travellers. A visitor who came at the end of the nineteenth century was Gregorovius, the German historian who wrote the monumental history of Rome in the medieval era. The Caetanis were one of the families – like the Colonnas and the Cenci – whose bloody feuds stained the pages of his book, and who had cluttered Rome with the medieval towers and churches which so embarrassed the republic of 1870.

Gregorovius came to Ninfa as a refugee from the new Rome. He had passed his adult life studying medieval parchments in the libraries of the convents, and was displaced in their appropriation by the new government as offices and barracks. The monks were expelled, and their manuscripts removed to a new and bureaucratic central depot. After four years of the republic he concluded that 'New Rome belongs to the new generation, while I belong to the ancient city in whose spellbound silence my history arose. Were I to come to Rome now for the first time, I neither should nor could conceive of such a work.'

At Ninfa he rediscovered that 'spellbound silence'. From a distance he saw

> a great ring of ivy-mantled walls, within which lay
> curious mounds and hillocks, apparently made of
> flowers. Grey towers stood up out of them, ruins, all
> garlanded with green, and from the midst of this
> strange circle we could see a silver stream hurrying forth
> and traversing the Pontine marshes. . . . I asked,
> amazed, what that most puzzling great garland of
> flowers, that mysterious green ring, could be. 'Nympha,
> Nympha' said our host. Nympha! Then that is the
> Pompeii of the Middle Ages, buried in the marshes –
> that city of the dead, ghostly, silent.

The moat had the potency of myth, its stagnant water as black and still as the River Styx. Giant carp wallowed in the reeds, fattened by centuries of isolation. Crossing the drawbridge he found the gate barred by a thicket of flowers; perhaps Gregorovius was himself a little feverish, but he imagined them to be straining to defend their sanctuary from any future violence:

> Flowers crowd in through all the streets. They march in
> procession through the ruined churches, they climb up
> all the towers, they smile and nod to you out of every
> empty window-frame, they besiege all the doors . . . you
> fling yourself down into this ocean of flowers quite
> intoxicated by their fragrance, while, as in the most
> charming fairy-tale, the soul seems imprisoned and held
> by them.

In the ruined church where Alexander III had been crowned the creepers parted to reveal mosaics depicting the Day of Judgement. At Pompeii, Gregorovius commented, the frescoes celebrated life and all its pleasures. Why was he so much more relaxed contemplating scenes of suffering and hell in this Pompeii *delle palude* – Pompeii of the marshes – than in the ossified, rectilinear city of stucco and ash? In this 'green kingdom of spirits' he experienced the momentary euphoria which came with the dissolution of individual identity into a flow of humanity and Time. Clumsy, shy, chafing, the wandering scholar from Neidenburg had not experienced a similar calm since his immersion in the archives of medieval Rome. But those manuscripts had been carted away, the interiors whitewashed, and their windows unbarred. Where could Gregorovius go next? It must have been very late in the evening when he returned across the drawbridge.

The marshes between the mountains and the sea – the Pontine marshes – were drained by Mussolini in the 1930s. What would Gregorovius see if he returned today? The Caetanis' tower and palace still stand, and the ground floor has been converted into a Heritage Centre which explains the social history of the community, complemented by displays of recent discoveries: pots, tiles, belt-buckles and a brooch. The frescos of the Day of Judgement have had to be removed to a museum for conservation reasons but can be seen in the store by appointment. The scaffolding in the nave is only temporary, and by way of compensation the repairs have revealed an arched door-lintel whose profile suggests that this church incorporated masonry from the late Byzantine period. The walls are stronger than ever, capped by cement; it is dangerous to climb on to the battlements, of course, but an asphalt path winds through the city and returns to the car park in less than half an hour. And do not walk on the grass.

I lie. If Gregorovius returned today he would find his 'green kingdom of spirits' as lush and mysterious as ever. Ninfa was rescued from modernity by an Englishwoman named Ada Wilbraham who married Prince Onario Caetani; in the 1880s she began to create an informal 'English-style' garden in the ruins, planting trees and shrubs and flowers but not disturbing the soil or the stones. Archaeologists were banned. Ada's spirit is still alive, because her approach was continued by the next two generations of the family. The last Caetani was Lelia, who with her English husband established a foundation which opens the gardens to the public one weekend every month. Lelia was a painter who presided over an artists' salon which met in the palace. One member was the novelist Giorgio Bassani and the atmosphere inspired the melancholy walled garden in which the past suffocates the present in his masterpiece, *The Garden of the Finzi-Continis*. '*Oh distante isola del passato*,' 'Oh distant isle of the past,' he wrote of Ninfa.

I first visited in the spring. A photograph can only show an assorted rubble of stones patchy with vegetation. How to illustrate the abundance of blossom, the profligacy of flowers, the pregnant softness of earth which for six centuries has been undisturbed but for the roots of trees? The butchered families and their burned homes have been mulched into a soil of delirious fertility, and the sound of water is omnipresent. The nymph's spring bubbles from a grove of bamboo into a stream which races under a bridge past ruined mills to the city walls. The bridge is the most photographed vignette in Ninfa: a brittle arch of stone which is no more than a metre in width, cascading with flowers whose petals are splayed on the surface of the water. It is almost too pretty to be true; as if we are inside a glass paperweight, but the blur of white is shaken blossom not snow.

I swam under the bridge and have never tasted water so clean, as gaspingly fresh as pure oxygen. The water races with a speed that suggests it is thrilled to escape from its underground caverns into the sunshine; weeds strain to grip the gravelly bed, extended to the tips of their roots. Only when the stream rushes under the walls and into the fields beyond does it relax, slowly curling into lazy meanders. When I climbed out of the water, breathless and shivering – it was March – a party of Italians stood on the river-bank, dressed in English brogues and Barbour jackets. They stared with open mouths. '*Inglese*,' said one, and the others nodded, '*Si, inglese.*' The guide added, '*Loro sempre la problema. Sempre vogliono lasciare il grupo, e fare il picnic.*' They are always a problem. They always want to leave the guided tour, and have a picnic.'

But Ninfa has a diametrical opposite which is as depressing as she is invigorating: the town of Ghibellina in Sicily, devastated by an earthquake in 1968. I had never heard of the place but a sign on the motorway reading THE RUINS OF GHIBELLINA was too tempting to ignore. We turned off, but after 20 kilometres of a pebbly lane twisting through valleys which were fertile and cultivated but oddly bare of houses my wife was beginning to lose patience. 'What ruins are these anyway? More dead stones?' I was resigned to abandoning the diversion, when she saw on the hillside ahead a vast, shallow flow of white concrete. It was in the form of a triangle, pointing down the slope as if it were an avalanche petrified in mid-flow. In such a lush valley the pristine concrete was surreal, dazzlingly white in the midday Sicilian sun.

There was a car park, and a sign confirming that these were I RUDERI DI GHIBELLINA but no further explanation. The perimeter of the concrete – about 10 feet high – was pierced by narrow pathways, so we entered. At first we scrambled up and down the walls as if it were an adventure playground but as we walked further and further into the maze the blind white walls became sinister. The twisting and turning channels were oddly similar to wandering in the lanes of a medieval town. But, of course, that was the answer: this was the medieval town, and its ruins were encased in a concrete mould. I knocked on the walls, wondering if the dead were entombed inside. It was the first sound in the valley since we had arrived. There was no reply, but a lizard flickered into a chink where the concrete had blistered.

When we returned to the car we breathed deeply. At the next motorway junction the signs read GHIBELLINA NUOVA and we found a bold and brand-new town of apartment blocks spaced around playgrounds and public art. No one was visible, however; no one sat at the neat, gleaming tables outside the cafés. There was no visible life, no laughter or children's yelling to pop the numbness of old Ghibellina.

Later, all was explained. Ghibellina had been hit by the earthquake which devastated the south of Sicily in 1968. The devastation was so great that the town was abandoned, and the survivors were resettled in a new model town. Artists were invited to suggest how to monumentalise the tragedy and the winner was Alberto Burri, a 'land artist'. The shattered houses were levelled to a uniform height, boxed in by wooden planking, and the white molten concrete poured into the mould. The result is a powerful experience for the tourist, but what the Ghibellini think I never discovered; it was their siesta, after all. There was no evidence of a dialogue between old and new, and I wondered what hope a memorial of such anonymous sterility promised the survivors. The fields in the valley flourish but Nature will never revive under the impervious, suffocating concrete.

We drove onwards, passing through areas where the earthquake had been less devastating and settlements

Ghibellina. In 1968 the town of Ghibellina, in Sicily, was destroyed in an earthquake. As a memorial to the dead, its ruins were encased in concrete by the sculptor Alberto Burri.

rebuilt. It is interesting how rarely people abandon their cities after natural disasters: Lisbon, San Francisco, Anchorage in Alaska, Managua in Nicaragua. Even Hiroshima was resettled in a hurry, survivors returning before they knew what the effects of radiation would be. In Sicily in 1693 an earthquake flattened forty towns. Eight of these were rebuilt on new sites in a style of glorious Baroque: domed Ragusa, hexagonal Avola and golden Noto. It was Noto we reached that evening.

I insisted on visiting Noto Antica first, the old city in the mountains which was reached after following a winding mountain road for many miles. 'Dead stones. It's depressing,' announced Anna as soon as we passed under the medieval gate. She was right abut the day's second diversion. No wall was more than knee-height, and a recent forest fire had left every stone charred, every tree black and leafless. Deprived of Nature's magic wand the ruin was lonely and sinister, and we dashed to the new city by the sea.

The earthquake had struck the prosperous city of twelve thousand people on 11 January 1693, a Sunday morning. 'The soil undulated like the waves of a stormy sea', recorded an eye-witness, 'and the mountains danced as if drunk, and the city collapsed in one miserable moment killing a thousand people.' The survivors stayed to piece together the rubble of their homes until the Spanish viceroy – Sicily was then ruled by Spain – decreed that the city should be removed from its isolated mountain ridge to a more convenient site on a hillside above the sea. The people bivouacked in tents and wooden huts on the appointed site. It was breezy and spacious but with no fresh water; that summer three thousand died of the plague.

After five years a referendum was held and the majority voted to rebuild the ruins. But these were farmers and artisans, and the educated minority – the nobles, clergy and lawyers – put their faith in the economic potential of the new site. Two Notos competed for a while but in the end, inevitably, the poor had to follow the rich. Like a trail of ants lumbering under crumbs of bread they hauled the rubble of their homes down the winding mountain road; new stone for new houses was too expensive. By 1702 a government official reported that at Noto Antica 'One sees nothing but the ruins from the earthquake except for two very small forts made by a shoemaker and two brothers that live there.'

The new Noto was *barocco* – indeed, *barroccissimo*. It is a city of palaces designed with an operatic gusto, and convents whose bell-towers sway dizzily with swollen curves. Few ordinary homes are visible; it is a stage-set erected in honey-coloured stone. Each façade has a triumphal gateway as its entrance, each window an extravagantly carved frame and an iron balcony of the type known as *panciuta* – 'bellied'. The courtyards are handsome, immaculate, but silent. The city creaks with solitude.

The haunting emptiness has drawn many artists to Noto, most famously Antonioni in his 1960 masterpiece *L'Avventura*. Film guides invariably describe this 'a study in alienation'. A party of socialites on holiday off the Sicilian coast swim from their yacht, and a girl disappears. Her lover and her best friend elope to Noto. Has the girl drowned? We do not know. They kiss, and gaze past each other. Are they in love, or just alienated? We do not know. At the end of the film they stare over the rooftops of the empty city while church bells clang in every tower. For Antonioni Noto was the perfect vacuum, a city whose own gaze is intense, beautiful and empty.

When we arrived a wooden platform had been erected in the square below the cathedral. There was a performance of dance tonight: a teacher of Latin dance had been in the city for several weeks, and as a farewell his pupils would demonstrate their new steps. The Netini filled the square. Smiling, plump and talkative, they appeared not to realise that artists had declared their city a necropolis, and its inhabitants ghosts. The teacher's capped heels clicked on the marble paving stones. In a crowd of swarthy, stocky Sicilians he was tall, slender and marvellously effete, and adored by pupils from girls of ten to men of sixty. After the individual performances the audience left their seats to dance a traditional Sicilian number. Midnight chimed from the cathedral tower, and they danced on in a trance of moonlight and marble and squeaky, blaring music from the gramophone. I was mesmerised by the rows of dark eyes sparkling in concentrated satisfaction. The formation moved forward and back, and back, and back, until I seemed to see the light in their eyes receding, and the waves of Netini dancing towards death, vanishing into the shadows to leave us alone in this beautiful, vacuous and suddenly terrifying city. Why such sadness in the face of such shared happiness? But it had been a long day, with too much sun.

# V

# An Exemplary Frailty

' I was angry as hell when they took away my title. But when you stand in the Pincio Gardens at sunset looking down on the whole of Rome, across centuries, it sorta puts things in perspective.' 'Marvellous' Marvin Hagler lost his world middleweight title to Sugar Ray Leonard in Madison Square Garden in 1986 through a referees' decision which is still argued over by boxing fans today. First Hagler hit the bottle, but then he moved to Rome and became the popular TV detective 'Sergeant Iron'. The boxing champion is the last of many proud kings who have come to Rome and been consoled by the sight of a far greater fall.

When the Vicomte de Chateaubriand visited Tivoli, a few miles south of Rome, he saw the signatures inscribed by earlier travellers in the chambers of the Emperor Hadrian's villa:

Many travellers, my predecessors, have written their
names on the marbles of Hadrian's villa; they hoped to
prolong their existence by leaving a souvenir of their
visit in these celebrated places; they were mistaken.
While I endeavoured to read one of these names,
recently inscribed, which I thought I recognised, a bird
took flight from a clump of ivy, and in so doing caused

several drops of water from the recent rain to fall: the
name vanished.

This prospect of oblivion cheered rather than saddened
Chateaubriand who was writing his *Génie du Christianisme*
(1802) as a manifesto for the revival of Christianity in France
after its abolition in the French Revolution. In the
Colosseum he discovered that the hermit whose bell once
tolled in the silence had died: 'It is thus that we are warned
at each step of our nothingness; man goes to meditate on
the ruins of empires; he forgets that he is himself a ruin still
more unsteady, and that he will fall before these remains
do.'

In Christianity the decay of the individual was a necessary
prelude to resurrection. Ruins were a perfect metaphor for
this process, for the skull beneath the skin; the more
magnificent the edifice, the more effectively its skeleton
demonstrated the futility of mortal pride. Rome's ruins were
a *memento mori* on a colossal scale. When in 1462 Pope Pius
II introduced the very first law to protect the classical
monuments from destruction, one of his reasons for doing
so was to preserve the sight of their 'exemplary frailty'.

For the greater part of the two millennia, Christian
visitors to the city were as uplifted as Chateaubriand by their
encounters with ruins. On their way to the shrine of St
Peter's pilgrims passed the mausoleum of Emperor Hadrian,
the great cylindrical drum on the River Tiber which had
been converted into the papal fortress of Castel Sant'
Angelo. What could be a more resounding statement of
futility? In *Urne-Burial* of 1658 Sir Thomas Browne
considered a mound of earth 6 feet in length to be as good

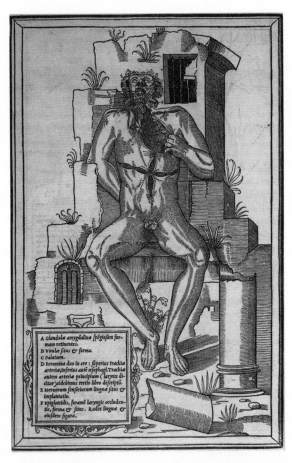

Etienne de la Rivière's woodcut illustrates a textbook on anatomical dissection by Charles Estienne, published in Paris in 1545. In the sixteenth and seventeenth centuries, a ruin was a metaphor for the frailty of mortal man: 'the skull beneath the skin'.

a guarantee of immortality as the 'stately Mausoleum or sepulchral pile built by Adrianus in Rome'. A contemporary of Browne who was in exile from Cromwell's Commonwealth was James Howell, a Royalist who had first travelled to Italy on a secret mission to steal the secrets of the Venetian glass-blowers. The classical Grand Tour had begun by this date, but in his *Epistolae Hoelianae* of 1645 Howell admitted that he felt elevated by the ruins of the Colosseum and the temples:

> Truly I must confess, that I find myself much better'd
> by it; for the sight of some of these ruins did fill me
> with symptoms of mortification, and make me more
> sensible of the frailty of all sublunary things, how all
> bodies, as well inanimate as animate, are subject to
> dissolution and change, and everything else under the
> moon.

Salvator Rosa wrote:

> All our works fall and sicken,
> Nothing is eternal:
> The Colossei die, the Baths,
> The worlds are dust, their pomp a nothing . . .

The poem is one of innumerable variations upon a theme put into verse by Petrarch, by Tasso and, most succinctly, by Jacques Grevin in *Le Bruit Ruineux* (1570):

> [Rome] crie en déclarant sa ruine publique
> Que rien n'est éternel que le grandeur de Dieu.

And it was as symbols of Christian victory that the artists of the Italian Renaissance began to paint classical ruins. Tumbling classical monuments in the backgrounds of masterpieces such as Pollaiuolo's *Martyrdom of Saint Sebastian* and Botticelli's *Nativity* are there to symbolise the shattering of the pagan world at the moment of Christ's birth, and the victory of the martyrs over their murderers.

Rome grieving. Fifteenth-century illustration. In the Middle Ages and the Renaissance Rome was personified as an eloquent corpse, a giant's body broken into pieces by its enemies or a mournful widow, as here in Fabrizio degli Uberti's poem *Il Dittamondo*.

The analogy between human and architectural decay explains why Rome is personified in human form in the Middle Ages and the Renaissance. In Fabrizio degli Uberti's thirteenth-century poem *Il Dittamondo* she is a neglected widow who guides the poet through her ruins, and in a manuscript of the poem illustrated with illuminated drawings the black-clad figure crouches sobbing inside the walls of the miniature-scale city like a child lost in Legoland. In Joachim du Bellay's sonnet-sequence *Antiquités de Rome* of 1557 the city is a speaking corpse and to Montaigne a few years later Rome was a body disfigured and broken into pieces by its enemies, who 'finding that, even though prostrate and dead, its disfigured remains still filled them with hate and fear . . . buried the ruin itself'. A recent advertisement for *Men's Health* magazine showed a muscular torso and asked, 'Is your body a temple or a ruin?'

In Britain it is in the seventeenth century that ruins become a popular metaphor for the decay of an individual life. As Roger Bowdler, the expert on the skull in art, explained in a definitive essay on the subject:

> The 17th century was a solemn and serious age; from
> whatever religious standpoint, its outlook was dour and
> anxious. The period's prolonged crises and widespread
> wars were combined with a philosophical outlook that
> emphasized man's imperfections rather than his dignity
> and potential, and concentrated more on his short-lived
> place within the Great Chain of Being. As a result, ruins
> had a positive meaning for the earth-bound mortal, and
> structural collapse provided a strong metaphor for
> death. All flesh is grass: man must wither and die, before

the soul can escape and return to God. . . . The Jesuit
martyr Robert Southwell likened dying in a devotional
work *The Triumphs over Death* of 1596 to demolishing
your old, rotten house in order to build a new and more
handsome edifice: 'withdraw your eies from the ruine of
this cottage, & caste them upon the majestie of the
second building'.

Or, as William Drummond wrote in *A Cypress Grove* of
1623:

By death we are exiled from this faire cittie of the world,
it is no more a world to us, nor we any more people in
it. The ruins of Fanes, Palaces and other magnificent
Frames, yeeld a sad prospect to the soul. . . . This Globe
environed with aire, is the sole region of death, the
grave where everie thing that taketh life must rotte, the
stage of Fortune and Change, onelie glorious in the
unconstancie and varying alterations of it.

Decay was necessary for every individual; conversely,
when the Last Trump sounded the end of Time all human
edifices would collapse, from the peasant's thatched cottage
to the emperor's shining dome. An astonishing scene of the
Day of Judgement visualised in toppling columns and
obelisks is carved on a table-tomb in the churchyard of St
Mary's, Lambeth, inside which in 1662 John Tradescant
was buried beside his father, also called John. The two
Tradescants were collectors of natural curiosities and
gardeners, and imported the plane-tree to Britain. The
epitaph read:

These famous Antiquarians that had been
Both Gardeners to the Rose and Lily Queen,
Transplanted now themselves, sleep here; and when
Angels shall with their Trumpets waken men,
And fire shall purge the World, these hence shall rise
And change their Gardens for a Paradise.

On the opposite face of the tomb the artist depicted the garden created by the elder Tradescant beside the ruins of St Augustine's Abbey in Canterbury. This is the earliest representation of the Day of Judgement in churchyard sculpture, Bowdler discovered. It was only at the very end of the Tudor reigns that painters began to introduce ruins into the backgrounds of their society portraits. They were metaphors of the inevitability of the subject's death; the grandfather of the nobleman who is portrayed with a ruin in his back garden would have been depicted with a skull in his hand.

But should the metaphorical ruin be Gothic or classical? Edmund Spenser was the first to transplant the imagery of Rome to English soil. His translation of Du Bellay's *Antiquités de Rome* was published in 1590, in his volume *Complaints: containing sundrie small poems of the Worlds Vanitie*. In the same volume were his lines on Verulam, in which the ruins of the city – like Du Bellay's Rome – lamented their fallen state:

Though nought at all but ruines now I bee,
And lye in mine owne ashes, as ye see:
Verlame I was; what bootes it that I was
Sith now I am but weedes and wastfull gras? . . .

High towers, faire temples, goodly theaters,
Strong walls, rich porches, princelie pallaces,
Large streetes, brave houses, sacred sepulchers,
Sure gates, sweete gardens, stately galleries,
Wrought with faire pillours, and fine imageries,
All those (O pitie!) now are turnd to dust
And overgrowen with blacke oblivions rust.

When Francis Bacon was raised to an earldom he chose
Verulam as his title in order to balance the acquisition of
worldly glory with a reminder of its transience; it is hard to
imagine a newly ennobled courtier making such an eloquent
choice today. Spenser overlaid the splendour of ancient
Rome as imagined in engravings and tapestries on to the
antiquities uncovered by farmers' ploughs in the fields
around St Albans. The only problem was that the low brick
walls and clay pots were utterly unimpressive to anyone who
had glimpsed the real Rome. Despite a century of busy
excavations they still are, and it took my own interest in the
ancient world a decade to recover after a visit at junior
school. The mighty Roman wall was slightly higher than the
wall around my grandfather's rose beds; an education officer
stood in the trench and rattled replica Roman weapons in a
didactic frenzy; no, boys, don't climb on the wall, barked
our teacher. But Verulam was the best England could do for
a Roman city; the Baths of Bath were yet to be discovered,
and Silchester was simply a pattern of streets imprinted into
a cornfield.

Quickly, the poets found a new source of *vanitas*: the
ruins of the eight hundred medieval abbeys which had been
seized, plundered and sold by Henry VIII. Their gaunt but

lonely stone skeletons littered the countryside and towns like the bones of dinosaurs. To the ordinary passer-by their ruins seemed as raw, bare and painfully explicable as bomb sites are to the modern age, and their first admirers saw an appeal to the soul rather than the eye. These were the 'antiquarians' who appeared in the landscape early in the seventeenth century, travelling historians such as Anthony à Wood of Oxford. When he visited the abbey at Eynsham in 1677 he noted in his diary: 'W. spent some time there with a melancholy delight in taking a prospect [making a sketch] of the ruins of that place. . . . The place hath yet some ruins to show, and to instruct the beholder with an exemplary frailty.' At the age of twenty-seven William Dugdale, the future author of *Monasticon Anglicanum* (1655–73), wandered through Osney Abbey, on the outskirts of Oxford. He meditated in his diary: '*Quid digni feci hic process. Viam?*' 'Truly nothing; only umbrages, Osney abbey ruines, etc., antiquities.' Osney is now vanished, and only commemorated by the name of a lock on the River Thames.

The first poetic appreciation of Gothic ruins in English literature is in John Webster's *The Duchess of Malfi* (1617), when Antonio and Delio meet in an ancient cloister. The play is set in Italy, but it is obvious that Webster has an English abbey in his mind. The cloister, says Delio:

> Gives the best echo that you ever heard
> So hollow and so dismal, and withal
> So plain in the distinction of our words
> That many have supposed it is a spirit
> That answers . . .

> ANTONIO: I do love these ancient ruins:
> We never tread upon them, but we set
> Our foot upon some reverend history:
> And, questionless, here in this open court,
> Which now lies naked to the injuries
> Of stormy weather, some men lie interred . . .
> Loved the church so well, and gave so largely to't,
> They thought it should have canopied their bones
> Till doomsday. But all things have their end:
> Churches and Cities (which have diseases like to men)
> Must have like death that we have.
>
> ECHO: Like death that we have.
>
> DELIO: Now the echo hath caught you.

The echo isolates the eternal truth of mortality. It is tempting to see the scene of two caped men in an echoing, shadowy medieval cloister as 'Gothic literature' but this would be wrong: 'Gothic' in the sense of atmosphere and horror is an invention of writers such as Horace Walpole, 'Monk' Lewis and Mrs Radcliffe in the second half of the eighteenth century. Antonio and Delio belong to the same literary cult of melancholy as Anthony à Wood and William Dugdale, a cult exemplified in visual terms by the Dutch artist Jacob van Ruisdael's painting of *The Jewish Cemetery* of *c*. 1670. In the foreground are a barren tree and tombstones washed by the changing light of a storm, and our eye is led across a desolate heath to the splintered walls of a ruined building. Beyond the ruin rises a rainbow, however. Melancholy was not a mood but a lucid, thoughtful theological journey to a divine radiance in which all shadows of doubt and loneliness disappear. In the eighteenth century there are two changes in the perception of the scene depicted by Ruisdael. First – and as we shall see in the next chapter – artists discovered a surface beauty in the jagged silhouettes and rough textures of the ruin. Second, the intellectuals of the Enlightenment no longer trusted in God's rainbow as a resolution to the doubts of human life.

So what lay beyond? One person's answer can be found under the solitary stone arch which stands in the fields at

Jacob van Ruisdael, *The Jewish Cemetery*, *c*.1670. Ruisdael was the only painter of the Dutch Golden Age to give a moral and emotional content to his depictions of landscape.

Pickworth, in Leicestershire, not far from the A1. In 1817 John Clare, a self-educated cottager's son born in a poor cottage in Northamptonshire, and had eked a living as a jobbing gardener and a plough-boy before arriving in the lime-kilns at Pickworth, came here as a young man of twenty-four. He was scratching together the money – a single pound – he required to print a prospectus inviting subscriptions for the publication of his first poems.

The village itself had been sacked and pillaged in the Wars of the Roses, and its ruins quarried for stone. The only survival was the pointed archway which had been the entrance to the parish church. This stood in a wilderness of brambles, nettles and elder-trees, because the fields around were too knobbly with old foundations for the farmers to plough.

At the end of a long day in the kilns Clare crossed the wilderness to sit in the archway. There he wrote his 'Elegy on the Ruins of Pickworth'. The poem opens with an angry young man's sermon on the unfairness of the countryside he has traversed as an itinerant labourer:

> . . . vain extravagance, for one alone,
> Claims half the land his grandeur to maintain,
> What thousands, not a rood to call their own,
> Like me but labour to support in vain!

But the ruins of Pickworth are consoling, because they show that the rich man's mansion is equal to the poor thatched cottage in the divine justice which comes with Time:

Ye scenes of desolation spread around,
Prosperity to you did once belong;
And, doubtless, where these brambles claim the ground,
The glass once flow'd to hail the ranting song.

'Whatever is must certainly be just': that was the traditional consolation which Clare had been taught as a boy in church. But his growing doubt in divine justice is reflected in the poem's sudden change of direction, quickening near its conclusion with a desperate fear of extinction. 'There's not a foot of ground we daily tread . . . but holds some fragment of the human dead'.

Like yours, awaits for me that common lot;
'Tis mine to be of every hope bereft:
A few more years and I shall be forgot,
And not a vestige of my memory left.

As the shadows lengthened at Pickworth the field of brambles became a field of human bones, and it must have seemed that the sun would never rise again. There was no glimmer of resurrection. A Romantic, he had trusted in the victory of emotional instincts but beyond God's rainbow had discovered only oblivion. The buried subtext to Clare's 'Elegy on the Ruins' was his rejection by his true love, Mary Joyce. Clare met his future wife while working at Pickworth but in his heart 'sweet Patty of the Vale' never displaced Mary, a farmer's daughter in his childhood village. Earlier that summer her prosperous father had forbidden her to see the poor and strange-eyed boy, and Clare trudged away into the neighbouring country, until he found work in the lime-kilns. Mary was to remain his obsession, the subject of hundreds of poems written until days before his death. At the heart of the poem is the fear that if Mary forgets his existence, he will be extinct.

When Clare's poems appeared three years later he became a celebrity in literary London but in the following decade his moods and hallucinations amounted to a nervous breakdown. In 1841 he was incarcerated in an asylum, where he died in 1863. His trust in the new Romantic philosophy had led him into a lonely, dark wilderness.

For Sir Walter Scott, too, memories of a first, long-buried love were awakened in 1827 by an excursion to a ruined abbey. Scott was a Stoic, not a Romantic, however, as we are persuaded by A. N. Wilson's masterly study of his work: he disapproved of the Byronic pose of emotional self-revelation in a writer's publications. It is from his private diary that we know of Williamina Belsches, 'his first, perhaps his only, love', who, Wilson thinks, he never 'got over'. Scott met Williamina in the porch of Greyfriars Church in Edinburgh after a service one Sunday morning in 1790; she was fourteen years old, he nineteen. It began to drizzle and he walked her home under his umbrella; he walked her home every Sunday for the next three years. But Scott was just a trainee lawyer and too poor to marry the granddaughter of an earl. Williamina married a banker, and they never met again.

Williamina died young, in 1810; Scott's own wife died fifteen years later, by which time he was ill with rheumatism and close to bankruptcy, owing to his publisher's incompetence. He began to commit his meditations to a private journal, in which we read how in the summer of 1827 he and some friends travelled to St Andrew's, which he had explored with Williamina all those years before. The ruins had cooled.

> The ruins . . . have been lately cleared out. They had been chiefly magnificent from their size not the extent of ornament. I did not go up to St Rule's tower as on former occasions; this is a falling off for when before did I remain sitting below when there was a steeple to be ascended? But the Rheumatism has begun to change that vein for some time past though I think this is the first decided sign of acquiescence in my lot. I sate down on a gravestone and recollected the first visit I made to St Andrew's now 34 years ago. What changes in my fortune and my feeling have since taken place, some for the better, many for the worse. I remembered the name I then carved in runic characters on the turf beside the castle gate and asked why it should still agitate my heart. But my friends came down from the tower and the foolish idea was chased away.

If it were not for the journal we would never know of Williamina, of her exceptionally pale skin and damp hazel-coloured hair in the Sunday morning drizzle at Greyfriars. At this time Scott was writing novels with a furious haste in order to pay off his massive debts. Poems on Williamina would have sold in their hundreds of thousands, but Scott was too honourable a man to exploit their past intimacy:

> If I were either greedy or jealous of poetic fame – and both are strangers to my nature – I might comfort

myself with the thought that I would hesitate to strip myself to the contest so fearlessly as Byron does, or to command the wonder and terror of the public by exhibiting in my person the sublime attitude of the dying gladiator.

More affecting than the melodramatic pose of the hero slain by heart-break, however, is the thought of the rheumatic old man sitting alone on a gravestone and staring at the shadow of Williamina's name in the dew. Three months after his visit he began a correspondence with her mother. 'The very grave gives up its dead and time rolls back thirty years', he

admitted to himself, suddenly dizzy with the rush of memories.

In Clare and Scott the sadness of their inner reflections is intensified by the ruinous backdrop to the scene, as if the architecture is a sounding-board to amplify the emotions. A similar mood is evoked by Constable's painting of the ruins of Hadleigh Castle. His wife Maria died in the winter of 1828 and a few weeks later the painter was busy copying scenes of Roman ruins; then his mind turned to the ruins of the thirteenth-century castle on the shore of the Thames estuary, which he had visited during their courtship fifteen years before. It was the first picture he exhibited as a Royal

*Hadleigh Castle* by John Constable, 1829, painted a few months after the death of his wife Maria.

Academician in the annual show, and the blackest canvas of his career; the castle tower is utterly broken.

This is not purely a question of stage-scenery, of lighting, silhouette and texture. There is also a vestigial *vanitas*, a lingering fear that these cold, smashed and lifeless stones represent extinction. The two elements are combined in Thomas Hardy's *Tess of the D'Urbervilles*.

Angel, Clare and Tess are honeymooning at Wool Manor, and on their arrival she tells her story of being raped by Alec D'Urberville. Angel withdraws into a cold, polite formality, thanks to a stubborn pride in his own intellectual conceptions; in the meadows that summer he had decided that Tess the dairy-maid was the embodiment of Nature's pure, fresh virtue. It is not until the early hours of their last night together that her bedroom door opens, and in a somnambulant trance Angel bundles Tess into a sheet and plants a full kiss on her lips. 'My poor, poor Tess – my dearest, darling Tess! So sweet, so good, so true. . . . My wife – dead, dead!'

Still asleep, he is drawn by some mesmerising force towards the dark silhouette of a ruined Cistercian abbey which lies in the fields across a bridge. The road is white in the brightness of the moon. Tess dangles limp with happiness, content to be a chattel, and content to drown in his arms if he loses his footing on the narrow plank which crosses the mill-stream. In the choir of the abbey church Angel places her shrouded body inside a stone coffin, and stretches himself out on the grass alongside. In Hardy's description it is as if a spot-light shines on the two figures, projecting their silhouettes in magnified form on to the wall behind. Tess's figure rises from the coffin and with infinite tenderness pleads with her husband to come home, lest he catch cold lying in his night-shirt in the dewy grass. The two figures stand upright and disappear, and Angel wakes in bed with his mind resolved. Later that day, he leaves her. The few minutes of the trance are Tess's only moment of happiness until the very end of the story, when for a few ecstatic days before her arrest and execution she and a humbled Angel are reunited in the solitude of a deserted, shuttered house. The ruins of the abbey amplify every beat of her heart, every whispered endearment, but the intensity of atmosphere is also the result of Hardy's own loss of faith.

Hardy's actual model was Bindon Abbey on the edge of the town of Wool in Dorset, which I visited one Saturday morning in the spring. The ruins stand in the garden of a manor house which was converted from the Abbot's Lodging, and they are no less romantic than when Hardy came. The mill-race is shredded into the same rivulets, and ivy and marigolds flow over the bases of the columns like seaweed on an old, barnacled pier. That May morning a white marquee had been erected on the grass inside the choir where Tess was laid, and a man at the gate explained that the owner's daughter was getting married that afternoon. It should be a sunny afternoon, we agreed. Inside the marquee a trumpeter began to practise his scales.

# VI

# Time's Shipwreck

Of the six hundred and fifty monasteries in England seized by Henry VIII in the 1530s, a third have disappeared under grass. Another third are in ruins, abandoned to the elements. The remainder were converted into houses, such as Bindon or Byron's Newstead, or into workshops or warehouses. The churches of a lucky few became cathedrals – St Albans, for example – or were acquired by the townspeople for their own use as parish churches; in Bath, the glorious Perpendicular structure was rescued in this way. There was not to be such a sudden change in the architectural landscape of Britain until the Second World War.

The monasteries were not demolished for the sake of it, although Thomas Cromwell's henchmen smashed as many icons as possible. The Crown seized the properties and sold their materials and their lands to the highest bidder. Not only did the monasteries own a quarter of the land in England, but stone and lead were highly valuable. Lead was a precious commodity, while quarries were few and far between and carting the stone long distances was far more expensive than its actual extraction. At Lewes in Sussex Cromwell gave the cloisters of the Convent to his son Gregory as a wedding present, but the church was demolished and its remains only discovered when the railway to London was cut through in the nineteenth century. Two 'plummers' from London were busy melting the lead, the site manager wrote to Cromwell in a letter remarkable for its dispassionate practicality. It was a question of measurements:

> The high altere, that was borne up with fower great
> pillars, having abowt it v chapelles . . . All this is downe
> a Thursday and Fryday last. Now we are plucking
> downe a hygher vaute, borne up by fower thicke and
> grose pillars . . . in circumference xlv fote.

Malmesbury Abbey in Wiltshire was bought from the agents of Henry VIII by a clothier named Mr Stumpe and converted into a woollen mill. When the antiquary John Aubrey visited in the 1660s the Norman nave still clattered with looms, and Mr Stumpe's great-grandson – Mr Stumpe, Esquire – plugged the beer-barrels in his cellar with wads of illuminated medieval manuscripts. 'The manuscripts flew about like butterflies,' wrote Aubrey in a plangent *vanitas*. 'All musick bookes, account bookes, copie bookes &c. were covered with old manuscripts . . . and the glovers of Malmesbury made great havoc of them. Before the late warrs [i.e. the English Civil War] a world of rare manuscripts perished hereabout.'

The opportunistic businessman and the melancholy antiquary were just two of the characters who passed through the ruins of the abbeys in the years following their Dissolution. In the course of three centuries straightforward greed was followed by ignorance and indifference, and curiosity led to veneration. The changes in attitude to ruins followed the same sequence as in Rome, but there the cycle required more than a thousand years to revolve.

Imagine an abbey in 1530, standing in cornfields or in a valley of the sheep-grazing uplands. Its bells toll the rhythm of the day, calling the villagers from bed and announcing prayer and noon and eventide. The monks are scholars illuminating manuscripts, or apothecaries tending the sick with herbs from their kitchen garden, or justices dispensing judgement in the courthouse – or, if you accept the reports by Henry VIII's agents, lazy gluttons who drink strong beer and stew on soft mattresses with the village slatterns.

Ten years later. The monks have been expelled, and wind and rain whistle through gate, cloister and choir. The soaring stone vaults of the church are picked clean like the rib-cage of a whale. The bells toll no more, sold to be melted down for their value as metal; the stained glass and the lead on the roof have also been sold for scrap. The villagers in their hovels suddenly have a quarry on their doorstep and stone walls replace those of timber and mud. Simple, squared blocks are most highly prized. The rounded drums of columns are only valuable as mill-stones, while ornamental capitals, pinnacles, or awkwardly shaped arches are of no use to anyone. This practicality explains the distinctive silhouette of the ruin.

The property has been bought from the king's agent by a local merchant. Sir John, recently knighted, settles into the abbot's private quarters which occupied one range of the cloister. He enjoys the great hall and its hearth but has the frescos covered with whitewash, their biblical imagery perhaps a little too challenging to see every morning. No one approaches the ruins with any curiosity for a century.

Then one day a quiet, pale gentleman rides over from Oxford and begins to pace over the ground with a pen and parchment, stopping to scrape away the moss and dirt on the coffins which lie in the nave. The villagers watch, puzzled: he is searching for treasure – what else? – but the silver candlesticks and chalice were sold and the abbots' coffins ransacked long ago. But the young man is not looking for treasure: indeed, he is more excited to discover a skeleton, or Latin words on a monument, or to uncrumple the manuscripts which cork the wine vats in the cellar of the manor. Torn leaves in hand, he paces the wild grass of the nave, staring at the sky as if he is trying to visualise what has disappeared. Did any of the villagers' ancestors pass down information about the abbey? No, they shrug. All they can show him is the carved lintel which forms the chimneypiece in the inn, and a broken-nosed angel used to wedge open the doors of the threshing barn. Why he curses the good king Henry VIII they cannot understand. Leaving, he pockets some shards of stained glass, and a fragment of a wall-painting which he will place in a corner of his rooms at Oxford. There had been no such curiosity when the abbeys were intact, an irony understood by John Aubrey: 'the eie and mind is no less affected with these stately ruines than they would have been when standing and entire. They breed in generous mindes a kind of pittie; and set the thoughts a-worke to make out their magnificence as they were in perfection.'

The antiquary is followed by an artist, early in the eighteenth century. He is a more convivial man, who laughs at the monks' skeletons and wears a broad felt hat which shelters him from the sun as he sketches in pencil. He is not interested in imagining what has disappeared, but he enjoys the way the light mottles the jagged, mossy stone, and the cattle munching their way across the foreground. For the villagers he is a new mystery: why paint this ruin? It is 'Picturesque', and he explains this novel word by indicating with his pencil the varied silhouette and jagged strokes of shadow. It is a pleasant change from painting the symmetrical, portico'd box which every gentleman seems to regard as a fashionable modern house. An architect enjoys symmetry, right angles and geometrical proportion but a painter does not. He has been commissioned by Sir John's descendant to paint views of his country manor to hang in the dining-room of his London house. Guests who dine at Grosvenor Square will admire how their host combines modern, classic taste with an ancient and honourable inheritance.

Design for landscaping at Esher Place, Surrey, by William Kent, *c.*1735. A flat agricultural landscape was transformed into Arcadia in Kent's design, inspired by the paintings of Claude and Poussin. Hills, trees and temples were created from scratch.

The next in line celebrates his marriage to a sugar planter's daughter by building a new house on a hill overlooking the ruins, sited where the artist had pitched his easel. The damp old Abbot's Lodging is let to a farmer. But the artist has cheated him, complains the owner, for the view of the ruin which is framed in his windows is less Picturesque than the scene in the painting. A landscape gardener is summoned, and he assures the family that the site has 'capability' for improvement: Nature's true beauty is latent, he explains, and like the proverbial angel in the block of marble can be extracted only by an artist. An army of labourers pitches camp in the ruins, and hundreds of shovels reveal the true beauty of the landscape. In the foreground the stream broadens into a glassy lake; hills rise to each side of the ruin, planted with trees whose dark foliage frames the scene. The horizontal bases of the arcades in the nave are buried, so that the columns seem to stand taller against the sky. The silhouette is still not quite right, however, and the designer dispatches a mason to hammer away until the wall is a little more rugged in profile. The mason is bemused, and so is the tenant farmer in the manor house. His herd of cattle is Picturesque, he is told, because they provide an element of 'movement' in the view from the house, their hides dappling with reflections as they graze at the water's edge. The slurry and hay do not belong in this Arcadia, however, and neither, unfortunately, does the farmer. The farmyard is relocated, and his front door is hidden from view. A new bridge is required for the widened river – but why not have it ruined? By this point the client is playing the game with gusto. The bridge is broken in two, and the void spanned by wooden planks. This elicits gasps and giggles from the ladies

who cross to picnic in the ruins and to sketch vignettes – a
column entwined with ivy, a doorway of monkish shadows
– which are passed around the drawing-room before dinner.

At the dawn of the nineteenth century, a young
architectural student stands and watches these picnics with
silent disapproval. He has the dust of London on his coat,
and in his hand a printed copy of the manuscript records
transcribed by the antiquary all those years ago. He
represents a generation of architects for whom these sites
have become sacred. Unable to travel to Italy because of its
occupation by Bonaparte, he began to explore the ruins of
his native countryside and fell in love with the 'bare, ruin'd
choirs, where late the sweet birds sang'.

He is a pupil in an architect's office in London. On his
drawing-board neo-classical columns are lined up like a row
of skittles. He is assisting in the design of a terrace of houses
in the suburbs, each porch a pair of Doric columns copied
from a page in a pattern book. That afternoon he will be on
site, arguing with the developer over the purity of the stucco
which is plastered on to the spindly columns of London
stock brick to give a semblance of stone. Sunday is his one
day free from this drudgery, and as soon as the office closes
on Saturday he takes a stage-coach to the countryside.

Its columns are six hundred years old, but underneath the
ivy and lichen they feel far more alive to him than the new
Hackney Doric. Each capital, each leering face or symbolic
animal, is different from the next in line; each has the
personality of its anonymous sculptor. This mason did not
dispute his payment; indeed, the architect cannot imagine
any exchange of coin in the construction of the abbey. The
pages of his Sunday sketchbook show that he is not

interested in the superficial and haphazard charms of the Picturesque; as if mentally undressing the ruin of its moss and ivy, he reconstructs the original design. The columns met thus; the rood screen stood here, painted and gilded in a multiplicity of colours. Here the choir sang; here was the library, and here the infirmary for the sick; beyond the mill-wheel turned. We have come full circle.

Now the vanished past has become an inspiration for the future, for the followers of the Gothic Revival saw the paternalistic society of the monasteries as the cure for the |ills of an industrialised society. The leading advocate of the Revival was the architect Augustus Welby Pugin, whose most easily recognised achievement is the neo-Gothic ornamentation he designed for the new Houses of Parliament. A devout Catholic polemicist who wore medieval clothes in his design studio, Pugin died hysterical and frustrated at the age of forty, in 1852. His novelty was to argue that the 'true' style of Gothic and the 'true' religion of Roman Catholicism were inseparable, and to blame the ills of modern society on the dissolution of the monasteries. In *Contrasts* (1836) he placed illustrations of past and present side by side. The bleak modern town is dominated by the prison, the poorhouse and the smoking factory chimneys, and its citizens are cogs in this industrial machine. The most succinct expression of Pugin's belief in the revival of 'Old England' is a model farmyard he designed at Peper Harrow in Surrey. Seen when driving along the watery valley of the Wey from Farnham to Godalming, the scene he created is as seductive as a mirage: a farmhouse, a barn high with hay and a gate lodge stand around a pond, each built in a muscular medieval style. The farm is placed on the site of a medieval abbey, the only remnant of which is a gabled end-wall pierced by the tracery of a window. Protected by Pugin with new buttresses and a defensive wall, this venerated relic was the symbolic centre of the new community.

Only a minority of his disciples were Catholics. *The Monastic Ruins of Yorkshire* (1843) is a collection of lithographs, the type one rifles through in a barrow on the Portobello Road. The introductory text written by the Rev. Edward Churton, an Anglican clergyman, is often discarded but explains the purpose of these images: Churton presents a description of Fountains Abbey and Rievaulx in their medieval prime in order to challenge the complacency of modern society. Had mankind been made happier by 'all the improvements of the nineteenth century . . . the new-found powers of machinery and steam, our Waterloo Bridge and chain pier across the Menai Straits?' Did the poor and elderly find the new poorhouses built on Benthamite principles as merciful as the refuge once provided by the abbeys, which were also 'the nurseries of education, the asylums of the afflicted, the seats of judicature, the record-offices of law? 'Our modern idea of freedom is to be subject to the fewest possible claims from the community.'

On a more positive note, Churton accepted that there had been a noticeable change in society's approach to the ruins themselves: 'Englishmen are no longer content to make mere excursions of pleasure to old sites, to spread their collation in the cloisters or aisle, and after a repast such as modern luxury can furnish, to rise up and abuse those pampered monks who passed their time in eating, drinking, and sleeping.' His picture might be drawn from one of

Fountains Abbey, photograph by Francis Frith, *c.*1859. The beauties of monastic ruins were rediscovered by poets and painters in the decade of the 1720s, and by the Victorian age the Gothic ruin was embedded in the romantic psyche.

the many guidebooks to Picturesque scenery published
fifty years before. The Rev. William Gilpin, for example,
concluded his description of Glastonbury Abbey with the
assurance that we view monastic ruins 'not only with a
picturesque eye, but with moral and religious satisfaction'
because they had been 'great nurseries of superstition,
bigotry, and ignorance: the stews of sloth, stupidity, and
perhaps intemperance'.

Yet it was these pampered picnickers who rescued our
medieval monuments from decay. The first attempt to
defend a medieval structure from demolition was made
for Picturesque not moral reasons, when in 1709 John
Vanbrugh tried to persuade the Duchess of Marlborough
to preserve the ruins of Woodstock Manor in the parkland
at Blenheim Palace. Vanbrugh was the architect of Blenheim, built as the nation's tribute to the late Duke of
Marlborough. In the foreground of the view from its
windows rose a new stone bridge with the widest span in
Britain, its epic scale designed to evoke the march of Roman
legions and, by analogy, Marlborough's victorious armies.
Across 'Pons Blenheimiensis' was the dilapidated Woodstock Manor, and the duchess naturally assumed that this
eyesore would be swept from view.

Vanbrugh wrote a letter giving two arguments for its
preservation. The first was its relationship to literature and
to legend. The manor house had been the trysting place of
Henry II and Rosamund Clifford, as celebrated in the old
ballad of 'Fair Rosamund'. Buildings of distant times 'move
more lively and pleasing Reflections (than History without
their aid can do) on the Persons who have inhabited them;
on the remarkable things which have been transacted in

them'. The second was its relationship to painting. If trees were planted on either side 'so that all the buildings left might appear in two risings amongst'em, it would make one of the most agreeable objects that the best of Landskip painters can invent'.

The plea was unsuccessful, not least because the duchess discovered a third reason which Vanbrugh did not admit in his letter – at her expense, he had furnished several rooms inside the manor as a *pied-à-terre* for himself. 'All that Sir J.V. says in his letter is false,' she marked in the margin. Woodstock was demolished, but this letter was a turning-point in English taste. Vanbrugh had suggested that a real landscape could be composed like a painted canvas, and that the audience could step through a picture frame into a living scene. Nature could be improved by the eye of the artist, who adds living trees and rocks, sunlight, water and old ruins to his palette.

This Picturesque way of seeing is arguably England's greatest contribution to European visual culture. Its influence was seen as far afield as the *jardins anglais* of Marie-Antoinette at Versailles or Catherine the Great's palaces, or the deliberate wildness of Central Park in New York. In 1812, during the French occupation of Rome, it was proposed to landscape the Forum in the 'English taste', framing each ruin with clumps of trees. Napoleon's fall put paid to the scheme, but it would have been the final triumph of English tourists' claim to understand Rome better than the Romans. Before the Picturesque movement, thatched cottages and creaking windmills were not considered worthy of a designed landscape, nor were Gothic ruins, or gnarled oak-trees, or old walls covered in ivy. It is because of this innovation that we buy calendars of countryside views, or those miniature ceramic models of cottages and water-mills. The Picturesque remains an inseparable element of English taste, although its last great exponent as an individual artist was John Piper (1903–82), who in 1941 wrote of how painting a brand-new house was as interesting as painting a young baby:

> There's one odd thing about painters who like drawing architecture. They hardly ever like drawing the architecture of their own time . . . I know perfectly well that I would rather paint a ruined abbey half-covered with ivy and standing among long grass than I would paint it after it has been taken over by the Office of Works, when they have taken off all the ivy and mown all the grass.

The Picturesque only had such profound influence in eighteenth-century England, however, because it was the artistic expression of the new 'philosophy of association'. At the beginning of the century beauty was judged by classical rules, and architectural design was based upon certain mathematical proportions. Perfect beauty was considered to be an objective quality, a configuration of geometry which was visible to the eye of a man of taste in the same way as musical harmonies were recognisable to an ear tuned by education. The Picturesque was the first aesthetic to suggest that beauty could be subjective, translating to the visual arts the theory that the mind works by the association of accumulated memories, as explained in John Locke's *Essay concerning Human Understanding* (1690). We associate smoke from a cottage chimney with the warmth of a fireside, for example, and castle turrets with the romance of chivalry – or Woodstock Manor with the ballad of 'Fair Rosamund'.

These subjective associations had their own logic, as argued by Edmund Burke in his *Philosophical Enquiry into the Origin of Our Ideas of the Sublime and the Beautiful* (1756). Certain encounters directed the viewer's thoughts towards 'self-preservation': a dungeon, a dark grotto, a chasm of black rocks, or Mount Vesuvius. These were 'Sublime'. A meandering river, the gentle slopes of a smooth lawn, or a classical temple in a grove of cypresses suggested ideas of 'self-perpetuation'. These scenes were 'Beautiful'.

Burke was only codifying reactions which designers of Picturesque gardens had understood and exploited for several decades in gardens such as Stowe in Buckinghamshire, Painshill in Surrey and Stourhead in Wiltshire. By the lake at Stourhead, for example, ladies were expected to shiver with horror as the path disappeared into a cold, dark grotto with a waterfall thundering in the invisible distance. Emerging into a gentle valley grazed by sheep they paused on the steps of a classical temple, and a gentleman in the party might be moved to declaim Virgil's *Georgics*. These country gardens were designed as circular walks deliberately punctuated by such incidents, and in the eighteenth century were opened to all respectable members of the public.

No one 'invented' the Picturesque. In retrospect, it can be understood as a confluence of philosophers, poets and painters whose ideas flowed in the same direction. Vanbrugh was a soldier, spy and playwright before he became an architect, William Kent a painter who designed the landscapes at Claremont and Stowe. Joseph Addison of

Magdalen College, Oxford, was a disciple of John Locke, and he applied his mentor's theories of cognition to aesthetics in a series of influential essays on 'The Pleasures of Imagination' written for *The Spectator* in 1712. Why, he wondered, did the experience of a Gothic interior reach recesses of the psyche which were untouched by classical harmonies? And why, when strolling in the meadows beside the Cherwell, did he find the untrimmed trees noisy with birds more liberating to the spirit than the topiary 'Cones, Globes, and Pyramids' in the formal, French-style gardens which were the established taste? 'I would rather look upon a Tree in all its Luxuriancy and Diffusion of Boughs and Branches, than when it is thus cut and trimmed into a Mathematical figure; and cannot but fancy that an Orchard in Flower looks infinitely more delightful, than all the little Labyrinths of the most finished parterre.'

The perfect example of the Picturesque sensibility was John Dyer, a painter, poet, farmer and country curate. At the same time as he trained in the studio of the painter Jonathan Richardson he began to describe landscape in verse. Begun when he was just sixteen years old, in 1716, 'Grongar Hill' described his walk up this hill in Wales, and how his feelings fluctuated in response to the changing views over the Aberglasney valley. The ruined castle on the summit of the hill was a concluding *vanitas*:

> And there the pois'nous adder breeds,
> Conceal'd in ruins, moss and weeds;
> While, ever and anon, there falls
> Huge heaps of hoary moulder'd walls . . .
> A little rule, a little sway,

A sunbeam in a winter's day,
Is all the proud and mighty have
Between the cradle and the grave.

Published in 1725 'Grongar Hill' was the first English poem to approach an actual landscape as a sequence of framed images. As with Vanbrugh, Dyer's originality can be explained by his leaping the boundaries between disciplines. It was as a painter that he travelled to Rome in 1724, where he wrote in a letter home:

> I am not a little warmed, and I have a great deal of poetry in my head when I scramble among the hills of ruins, or as I pass through the arches along the Sacred Way. There is a certain charm that follows the sweep of time, and I can't help thinking the triumphal arches more beautiful now than ever they were, there is a certain greenness, with many other colours, and a certain disjointedness and moulder among the stones, something so pleasing in their weeds and tufts of myrtle, and something in them altogether so greatly wild, that mingling with art, and blotting out the traces of disagreeable squares and angles, adds certain beauties that could not be before imagined, which is the cause of surprise no modern building can give.

Dyer has stumbled across a major discovery: a building can seem more beautiful in ruins than when its original design is intact. Dyer published his poem on *The Ruins of Rome* in 1740, by which time he was a gentleman farmer in Higham in Leicestershire. In a naturalistic garden ornamented by 'a rustic temple, a bower on a hill, and a Doric temple near the fish-pond' he fattened the sheep which would be the subject of his last great poem, *The Fleece* (1757), an adaptation of Virgil's *Georgics* to the woollen industry of modern Britain. Dyer was no eccentric but, in the parlance of the time, a 'man of feeling'. His passages of melancholy were, like a ruin seen by the wayside, passing episodes in a search for spiritual contentment, and the reconciliation of the virtues of classical antiquity with a nation of farmers, merchants and shopkeepers. While he was polishing *The Ruins of Rome*, he was simultaneously at work on a 'commercial map' for the improvement of Britain's inland navigation.

The first half of the eighteenth century was the springtime of the Picturesque. It was as if the corpses of abbeys and castles had been given a second life by artists and 'men of feeling'. In the 1720s John Aislabie, who as Chancellor of the Exchequer had been disgraced by the South Sea Bubble scandal and imprisoned in the Tower, was required to retire to his country estate. An 'outlaw myself and surrounded by impenetrable obscurity', as he joked to a fellow exile, he busied himself with transforming into a garden the rocky valley of the River Skell, which twisted and turned from the ruins of Fountains Abbey to his own house at Studley Royal. The site would have been rejected by a French garden designer, but its very wildness was a virtue in the decade of 'Grongar Hill'. Paths wound between pavilions placed on the outcrops of rock, and by the careful planting of trees Aislabie created a multiplicity of vistas framing temples across the valley, and focused on the statues and ponds placed on its grassy floor. After the second turn in the valley the silhouette of the 'Queen of British ruins' rose before your eyes. The abbey stood on a neighbour's land, in fact, but the visitors enjoying the vista were not to know.

Fountains was the first of several abbeys to be incorporated into the views from modern gardens. At Duncombe Park in Yorkshire, a grass terrace runs from a statue of Father Time on the lawns in front of the house to a rotunda on a distant promontory. The terrace was created in 1758 to allow views of Rievaulx Abbey in the Ryedale below, built on a curve so that the twelfth-century ruins are never seen from the same angle; in the viewer's eye they revolve like an object turning on a potter's wheel. Trees were planted to allow only occasional glimpses, and to Arthur Young riding over the turf in 1768 the flickering views through the trees were like glimpses into a magical kingdom. It was in the ruins of Rievaulx that Dorothy Wordsworth rested that evening in 1802, listening to the thrushes singing in the green hillocks.

Roach Abbey, again in Yorkshire, lay a mile from the Earl of Scarborough's newly-built house of Sandbeck Park. In the 1770s Capability Brown was commissioned to landscape the scene, agreeing in the legal contract 'to finish all the Valley of Roach Abbey in all its parts (With Poet's feeling and with Painter's Eye)'. A stream beside the cloisters became a cascade, and the low horizontal walls were grassed over in order to emphasize the verticality of the columns.

It was also in the eighteenth century that medieval castles began to be incorporated into Picturesque gardens. The Arundells' stronghold of Wardour Castle in Wiltshire was one of many ruined in the Civil War, and this battered, split hexagon of the greenish local stone preserves a certain poignancy. First, it was besieged by Parliamentarians: in Lord Arundell's absence his wife Blanche commanded an heroic but futile resistance. Arundell returned to recapture the castle, but was forced to tunnel into his own cellars and detonate a mine in order to expel the enemy. After the Restoration his descendants were too impoverished to rebuild, for as devout Catholics they were barred from holding public office. They lived in farmhouses on the estate, until the 6th Lord's advantageous marriage to the heiress to the land on which Soho was built – hence Wardour Street – enabled him to build New Wardour Castle in the 1770s. The house was in the latest neo-classical style but sited to enjoy views of the old castle from the windows of the saloon, for its ruin was a monument to the ancestry of the Arundells, to their loyalty to the king and to a persecuted faith.

Families whose estates were bare of antiquities could erect artificial ruins, and the two earliest can be dated to around 1729: a hermitage named King Alfred's Hall in Cirencester Park, and a sham church at Fawley Court, near Henley. More than thirty mock-ruins of abbeys and castles were erected in English landscape gardens in the eighteenth century, so I shall describe the example which for me encapsulates their charms and also their complexities: the sham castle at Wimpole Hall, near Cambridge.

Its architect was a gentleman amateur named Sanderson Miller who designed eye-catching follies for the estates of his friends, such as the castle at Lord Lyttelton's Hagley Hall (1747–8) which was described by Horace Walpole as bearing 'the true rust of the Barons' Wars'. Two years later Lyttelton wrote to Miller on behalf of Lord Hardwicke of

Design for a Sham Castle at Wimpole Hall, near Cambridge, by Sanderson Miller, *c.*1749–51. Miller was a country gentleman who never refused an invitation to visit a friend's estate and design an ornamental 'folly'.

Wimpole Hall, requesting a design from the 'Grand Master of Gothick':

> he wants no House or even Room in it, but mearly the Walls and Semblance of an Old castle to make an object from his house. At most he only desires to have a staircase carried up one of the Towers, and a leaded gallery half round it to stand in, and view the Prospect. It will have a fine Wood of Firrs for a backing behind it and will stand on an Eminence at a proper distance from his House. I ventured to promise that you should draw one for his Lordship that would be fitt for his Purpose . . . I know that these works are an Amusement to you.

Miller drew an impression of the castle on its wooded

knoll, and a series of elevations whose raggedness he sketched with the zest of someone tearing a piece of paper. Certainly, he used no compass or set-square. Construction did not begin until 1767, however, by which time Miller had gone mad. His drawings were handed to the landscape gardener Capability Brown and to an architect, James Essex. The end-result was a little solid, a touch too professional, complained Lady Hardwicke:

> The Tower is better for being raised, but the additions
> Mr Brown has quite changed from our plan, though he
> undertook to follow it and said he liked it. That is, he
> had 'Unpicturesqued' it by making it a continuous solid
> object, instead of a broken one. The wall . . . is
> continued entire at the bottom from the whole Tower
> to the Broken one, and is to be fractured only in the
> upper half of the Gateway.

In the 1990s a version of the Wimpole Folly was commissioned by John Paul Getty Jr. for a hilltop on his estate at Wormsley in Buckinghamshire, in order to conceal his satellite dishes. Did Lord Hardwicke also have a hidden agenda, beyond the natural desire to enliven a flattish East Anglian landscape? He was a parvenu, a lawyer from a middle-class family who rose to become Lord Chancellor and bought his country estate in 1740. Like an assumed coat of arms a castle on the skyline endowed his seat with an instant lineage. That is one suggestion. The castle has also been interpreted as a political symbol, noting the praise for 'manly Virtues of the Norman line' which is expressed in a poem dedicated to the folly: 'Free, hardy, proud, they brav'd their feudal Lord / And try'd their rights by ordeal of the Sword.' In a period preoccupied with the respective rights of monarch and Parliament, politicians in the Whig Party admired the barons of the Magna Carta as the defenders of English liberties. This political symbolism worked hand in hand with the Picturesque in the rise of appreciation for the nation's medieval heritage: at Stourhead, for example, the lakeside walk passed scenes of classical mythology while an outer circuit on the encircling hilltops encompassed monuments to defenders of British liberty, including a tower in the Saxon style which was dedicated to King Alfred.

There is a third theory, however. Hardwicke and Lyttelton were leading figures in the government which crushed the Jacobite rising of 1745, and in their propaganda they claimed that Bonnie Prince Charlie wished to restore the feudalism and superstition of the barbaric Gothic age. After the battle of Culloden it was Hardwicke, as Lord Chancellor, who put his signature to the Acts of Parliament that abolished the 'baronial' institutions which had survived north of the border. Did the ruin on the skyline remind him of his achievement in destroying the last traces of medievalism?

Whichever is the correct interpretation, the uncertainty demonstrates that 'Gothic' was a double-edged sword. The word had been introduced in the Renaissance as a synonym for 'barbaric' and for the majority of educated people in Georgian England it continued to be a term of opprobrium. When Byron swore that Lord Elgin was a worse vandal than Alaric the barb only struck home because of Britons' pride in being heirs to the ancient Romans.

In 1789 a parson named William Clubbe erected a pyramid in the garden of his vicarage at Brandon, in Suffolk. It was assembled from fragments of medieval wall monuments which had been destroyed in the modernisation of the church in the nearby parish of Letheringham. Infuriated, Clubbe had collected the wreckage and composed an epitaph in which the mutilated stones hurl a final insult at the neighbouring parson:

FUIMUS!
Indignant Reader! These Monumental Remains are Not
(As thou Mayest Suppose)
The Ruins of Time
But
Were Destroyed in an Irruption of the Goths
So late in the Christian Era
As the Year 1789
CREDITE POSTERI!!!

Clubbe's pyramid was not the first folly to use genuine fragments in order to comment on the vandalism of a supposedly civilised age. The first of this genre was also a vicar's private revenge on his peers. Recently ordained, the antiquary William Stukeley arrived in Stamford in 1730, his parish church of All Saints' being one of the many medieval churches whose spires grace the Lincolnshire skyline. His delight in the benefice was upset when he discovered that the vicars in the neighbouring churches were busy whitewashing medieval frescos, removing stained glass, and installing new, pinewood pews. Stukeley's protests were in vain, and his only consolation was the news that owing to

The hermitage at Stamford, drawn by William Stukeley. The hermitage built by the Rev. William Stukeley in his garden at Stamford, Lincolnshire, in 1738 was decorated with stained glass and sculpture rescued from local churches undergoing 'modernisation'.

the dazzle of the new glass the Rev. Popple of St Martin's was forced to wear dark spectacles when preaching – that, and being able to purchase a few colourful shards from the glazier who was carting away the smashed medieval glass. He installed these pieces in the windows of a mock-ruin built at the end of his garden, a composite of salvaged medieval fragments which was as fantastic, self-absorbed and fragile as a child's sandcastle. Like Clubbe's pyramid it has disappeared but its reappearance is recorded in Stukeley's own pencil drawing. It was a three-dimensional representation of Francis Bacon's metaphor: 'antiquities are history defaced, or some remnants of history which casually have escaped the shipwreck of Time'. Indeed, the course of Stukeley's life seems to illustrate that haunting image.

The hope of an impoverished genteel family, William had

matriculated at Cambridge at the age of sixteen, in 1703. He was a student of medicine but was seduced by ruins as an undergraduate, walking alone over the Fen meadows to 'sigh over the Ruins of Barnwell Abbey, and [I] made a Draught of it, and us'd to cut pieces of the Ew trees there into Tobacco Stoppers, lamenting the Destruction of so many monuments of the Piety and Magnificence of our Ancestors'. This adolescent loneliness was the beginning of a career in which he became Britain's foremost scholar of Druidic and Roman Britain. The sheer physical exhilaration of belonging to the generation which rediscovered ruins in the 1720s is evident in a memoir of his travels across the country. Staying at a friend's house in Northamptonshire his companion in exploration was the younger sister, a girl of 'an airy temper':

> she accompanyed me in several of my Rambles in that Country to view Antiquitys, Roman Camps, and the like. We traveld together like Errant Vertuosos, and when we came to an old ruind castle, etc., we climbed together thro' every story and staircase . . . pulling each other over the gaping arches and rugged heaps of rubbish, and when I had occasion to draw a view of them out . . . she held my ink horn or my paper . . . and all without reserve or immodesty; nor could any aged Philosophers have conversed together with more innocent familiarity or less guilt even than in thought or intention.

He was appointed to be the first secretary of the Society of Antiquaries at its foundation in 1717, and four years later he paid 4s. for wooden bollards which protected from road traffic the monument at Waltham Cross, erected by Edward I to commemorate where the body of his wife Eleanor had rested overnight on its way to Westminster Abbey. Returning in 1757 he was furious to discover that the commissioners of turnpikes had removed the bollards, in order to quicken the journeys of market wagons and stage-coaches. He ordered the construction of a brick wall, and in a public address lamented: 'with grief I discern us dropping into Gothic barbarism.'

Like John Dyer Stukeley was a 'man of feeling'; unlike Dyer, however, he fled the present day, escaping modern society and its speeding carriages to find a lonely solace in the fragments he could rescue from Time's shipwreck. Before Stamford he lived at Grantham, and, in 1728, in the garden he also created a hermitage which was a scrapbook of personal memories. Most oddly, after his wife miscarried:

> The embrio, about as big as a filberd, I buryd under the
> high altar in the chapel of my hermitage vineyard; for
> there I built a niche in a ragged wall overgrown with
> ivy, in which I placed my Roman altar, a brick from
> Verulam, and a waterpipe sent me by Lord Colrain from
> Marshland. Underneath is a camomile bed for greater
> ease of the bended knee, and there we enterred it,
> present my wife's mother, and aunt, with ceremonys
> proper to the occasion.

In the Stamford hermitage he included a small niche with room to seat one person only. I imagine that he re-created the introspective solitude of Barnwell Abbey, smoking a pipe and perhaps – like the man in his garden shed in cartoons from the 1950s – hiding from his wife. 'Stukeley, it is well-known, married Discord', wrote a historian of the time.

There is a more imposing 'folly' ruin built on marital discord: the Jealous Wall at Belvedere House in Ireland, on the shores of Lough Ennell. Erected *c.*1760 by Robert Rochfort, Lord Bellfield, the jagged stone wall is 180 feet in length and the height of a three-storey house, and was designed to appear to be crumbling from the parapet downwards. In 1736 Bellfield had married, at the age of twenty-eight, a sixteen-year-old girl from Dublin named Mary Molesworth. He spent much time in London, where he was prominent in the representation of Irish affairs at court. Left alone with the children, Mary fell into the arms of her young brother-in-law, Arthur. Bellfield discovered her infidelity; she confessed, and Arthur took to his heels. The courts awarded Robert £20,000 damages and poor Arthur died in the debtors' prison. Robert placed Mary under house arrest for the next thirty years, and forbade any visitors but their children. He once encountered her in the gardens without warning, and was so upset that he instructed a servant to walk in front of her in future, ringing a bell. Mary was released at her husband's death in 1774, but she had long since gone mad.

Bellfield built the Jealous Wall to block the sight of the house where his wife had been seduced; it is a bitter inversion of the romantic vista suggested by Vanbrugh for Fair Rosamund's Woodstock Manor. That is the legend; the truth is more mundane. Robert built the wall in order to conceal from view the house of a second brother, George, with whom he had quarrelled about money. The interest of a ruin rarely lies in its reality. But tell that to the council official who erected a sign in front of a Gothic folly in a park in Abingdon. Sightseers beware, the sign read: THESE ARE NOT REAL RUINS.

# VII
# Serious Follies

There is one place in Britain where you can sit on a toppled Roman altar to meditate, and listen to birdsong in a forum of ancient marble: Virginia Water in Surrey. Beside the placid lake are the colonnades of a ruined city. Approach closer and you find an old sign inscribed with admirable perfunctoriness:

These Ruins were erected on this site in 1827
by King George IV
having been imported in 1818
from the Roman city of Leptis Magna
near Tripoli in Libya
DANGER – KEEP OUT

Thirty-seven tall columns of marble and granite stand shivering in the damp valley, having exchanged the sun and sand of Africa for the damp moss of Surrey. They seem as unaccustomed to the ferns underfoot as we are to scorpions, as glum in their exile as the Blackamoor footmen who were so fashionable in European palaces of the time. Why did the columns of Leptis Magna come to Virginia Water?

They form the largest artificial ruin in Britain and, like that of the Elgin Marbles, their journey was motivated by a combination of cultivated taste, patriotism and political opportunism. In theory, the ruins were a diplomatic gift from the Bashaw of Tripoli to the Prince Regent; in practice, consent was tickled from the Bashaw by the consul-general in Tripoli, a Colonel Warrington who was anxious to further his career. In 1816 he visited the site of the Roman city with its great Forum built by Emperor Septimius Severus in AD 200. With him were Captain Smyth, a naval officer, and Augustus Earle, an artist. Earle's water-colour in the Royal Collection at Windsor Castle shows how the dunes of the Sahara had drifted over the city abandoned after the Vandals' invasion in the fifth century, and his notes recall how the fine, light sand had preserved the fragments perfectly.

Warrington was permitted to give to the Prince Regent whatever he could extract from the sand. Two years later thirty-seven of the forty columns, ten capitals, twenty-five pedestals, ten pieces of cornice, five inscribed slabs of sculpture and some fragments of sculpture arrived in England. The three tallest columns could not be fitted on board the ship, and were left lying on the beach at Leptis; they remain there today, prostrate and forlorn.

The ruins cluttered the forecourt of the British Museum for eight years; no one quite knew what to do with the Bashaw's tribute. Finally, it was suggested that they be re-erected as a 'folly' in the royal family's private estate at Virginia Water. The pieces were removed by the Royal Engineers, travelling on gun-carriages down Oxford Street, recently surfaced with the new 'tarmacadam', and on across Hounslow Heath. The king's architect Jeffrey Wyattville was faced with a disorderly pile of fragments from which he had to create a building. There are no design drawings, and no doubt he improvised; there is a playful fragility in the assembly, as if tipsy giants had been playing with colossal Lego.

The obvious solution would have been to build a podium and position the thirty-seven columns as the peristyle of a temple. Wyattville was cleverer. First, he chose as his site a shallow valley running down to the water's edge and spanned by a brick road-bridge. Second, he created an architectural space – or, put another way, the experience of walking through a ruined city. From the landing-stage at the water's edge, where in 1828 the Prince Regent – now George IV, and so fat that he could only waddle – arrived to inspect the folly, we stroll between the two colonnades, under the bridge and into a semicircular temple. Wyattville

In 1827 the ruins of Leptis Magna, Libya, were re-erected in the gardens of King George IV at Virginia Water.

reserved the tallest marble columns for this climax; the Picturesque relied upon the sudden contrasts created by shadows, concealment and surprise.

To frame the scene in the valley he erected walls of new, battered stone and embellished the brick road-bridge with a chipped cornice so that it assumed the appearance of an archway in a city wall. Strolling through the ferns we imagine that the valley has filled with the sediment of centuries, and wonder what treasures lie concealed below the damp earth. In fact, Wyattville lacked pedestals: twelve of the columns had come without their bases, because of the depth of the Libyan sands. He relied upon his audience to imagine what was missing: that is a rule of the game. A ruin is a dialogue between an incomplete reality and the imagination of the spectator; as they strolled between the colonnades his visitors would recall the Roman Forum, Ephesus, or Palmyra, each completing a picture of their own. His solution is masterly, perhaps more imaginative than the design of Leptis Magna itself.

The enthusiasm for erecting mock-classical ruins was at its strongest in France, Germany and Britain but the first were erected in Italy itself – perhaps surprisingly, given the quantity of real ones available. The earliest record is of a two-storey house in the Duke of Urbino's park at Pesaro of *c.*1530, designed by the architect Girolamo Genga. This has disappeared and the earliest surviving artificial ruin – under scaffolding at the time of writing – is a bridge by Bernini at the Palazzo Barberini in Rome. Two arches cross the moat between an ante-room in the palace and the garden. The first is built as if the keystone has slipped; the second has collapsed but a wooden drawbridge is lowered in its place.

The composition was meant to give a playful *frisson* to the guests of Cardinal Barberini, perhaps when strolling into the gardens after lunch. As a termination to the vista across the bridge he proposed to re-erect a Roman obelisk which lay fractured in the courtyard.

Such patrons consciously saw themselves as turning the wheel of resurgence: Rome reborn. A rejected design for the Trevi Fountain in 1730 proposed to decorate the wall behind the fountain with a painted scene of the ruined aqueduct of the Acqua Virgo from Tivoli. The comparison of this backdrop to the gushing fountain in the foreground would have celebrated the Popes' achievements in restoring the supply of water to Rome. Thus, a ruin is placed in juxtaposition with a new building in order to tell a story, a dynamic version of 'before' and 'after'.

Rome's most beguiling artificial ruin is under lock and key, guarded by the nuns at the Convent of Santa Clara at Sta Trinità dei Monti. It is a monk's cell painted in the 1760s in *trompe-l'oeil* by the French artist Charles-Louis Clérisseau in order to represent the interior of a ruined temple. For a very long time this room was known only by the design drawings and it was assumed to have disappeared, but in the 1960s it was discovered intact by the art historians John Fleming and Thomas McCormick. The convent is reached by climbing the Spanish Steps, and entering the cloister to the side of the famous twin-towered façade of Sta Trinità dei Monti. Keys jangling in the silence, a nun leads a visitor through endless shuttered corridors, with a slow patter which is both proud and coy. At last, a plain metal door opens into the 'Ruin Room'. I had studied the design drawing at the Fitzwilliam Museum, Cambridge, and the

Design for the Ruin Room at Sta Trinità dei Monti, Rome, by Charles-Louis Clérisseau, *c.*1766, decorated in *trompe l'oeil*, imitating a Roman temple which had become the residence of a Christian hermit.

cell was a fraction of the size this perspective view suggested, but the *trompe-l'oeil* on the walls was as fresh and colourful as in the original water-colour. Today an electric light-bulb dangles from a ceiling in which painted rotting planks split to reveal a blue sky; a bright red parrot perches on a beam. We are standing inside a Roman temple, and see countryside between the columns. The abandoned *cella* has become the home of a Christian hermit, his furniture improvised from the crumbling fragments. As Legrand described:

> the vaults and several portions of the wall have fallen
> apart and are held up by rotten scaffolding which seems

> to allow the sun to shine through . . . the [fireplace] is a
> mixture of diverse fragments, the desk a damaged
> antique sarcophagus, the tables and chairs, a fragment
> of cornice and inverted capital respectively. Even the
> dog, faithful guardian of this new style of furniture, is
> shown lodged in the debris of an arched niche.

The room was made for Father LeSueur, a monk who was also a mathematician of distinction. One *trompe-l'oeil* book is lettered NEWTON on its spine. This was his bedroom and study and we can only speculate as to why he chose to live in ruins; was it, I wonder, a reminder that his scientific studies were only a particle of dust in God's scheme? The artist Charles-Louis Clérisseau was a professional 'ruinist', the author of more than a thousand drawings of ruins. Many of these were *capricci* – playful assemblages of real fragments – and many a record of actual locations. Although he aspired to be an architect his temperament was too unstable, and he completed few commissions. He was used as a ruins consultant, advising on interiors and garden follies. Talking to him was like opening the door of an ancient tomb and breathing the ancient odour, as the art historian Winckelmann noted. 'I very much hope . . . that the noxious modern air that you are going to breathe does not invade your new productions', he wrote when Clérisseau departed Rome for Sala, near Venice, where he had been commissioned to design a garden in the style of an emperor's ruined villa for the Abbé Farsetti. There would be a private amphitheatre, a house-cum-museum for the client, and a Roman road lined with tombs and sarcophagi. Beside this new Appian Way would be a canal crossed by an ornamental bridge, and the abbé's vista would be terminated with a monument 100 feet high. This would have been the most impressive folly in Europe, but after a prototype 15 feet high had been carved in cork Clérisseau buckled at the immensity of the task and escaped to France.

Clérisseau captivated the British students who came to Rome in the 1750s, including the two who would become the great rivals of their generation: Robert Adam and William Chambers. Adam captured the imagination of London society with his dazzling Pompeian interiors, helped by his cynical exploitation of Clérisseau's expertise. The ruinist, he told his brother, could be persuaded to follow him to Britain for just £150 to £200 a year: 'Though a French man he has no Allegria or Company, nor no thoughts of Eclat or Ambition. Thus though sensible of his own Merit (which is infinite) yet he may be managed like a lap dog.' William Chambers, by contrast, was a friendlier man than Adam, kindlier to his assistants, and in his old age fond of singing Swedish love-songs at Royal Academy dinners. He tutored George III in architecture and designed Somerset House for civil servants but his outward appearance of neo-classical correctitude concealed a subversive imagination. Chambers played the ruins game better than the more fashionable Adam, and three of his designs were the most daring experiments of their time.

Swedish by birth, Chambers had travelled to China and studied as an architect in Paris. He befriended the French students also on scholarship at the Académie Française and sketched the city's ruins on excursions with painters and sculptors. This interaction with other disciplines was a humbling but liberating experience for a professional architect, for Chambers quickly learned that the lucid, rational solutions of the design studio are only the first chapter in the story of the building. Legrand described how at the announcement of any new excavation the young students at the Académie would run to the site, and 'when the workers in marble came to search the debris for something to make a base, a bust, a vase, and disarranged the picturesque disorder of the fragments, our two antiquaries called these *barbarian incursions into their realm*'.

A few months after Chambers arrived in the city in 1751 news came of the sudden death of Frederick, Prince of Wales. Chambers designed a mausoleum to commemorate him in the gardens of the Prince's palace at Kew. There was little chance of the design ever being built, but he put pencil to parchment in the same way that a poet might write a eulogy. The concept of a mausoleum in a landscape was a revival of the Roman practice of burying dead citizens outside the city walls, as exemplified by the Appian Way. *Siste Viator*, the inscriptions command: pause, traveller, and reflect on the virtues of the occupants. Later, Chambers was to propose the erection of the tombs of British heroes along the Bayswater Road.

In a unique innovation, Chambers made a second drawing in which he imagined how the structure might appear as a ruin in years to come, with fir-trees rooted in the fissures of its shattered dome. The drawing has puzzled scholars. Is its ruinous condition simply a device to reveal the cross-section? Was it intended to be built as a ruin, or was Chambers simply speculating on the effects of decay on a solid structure? Perhaps there was also a moral message.

Admirers of the antique saw the survival of ancient mausoleums as illustrating the triumph of virtue over Time, and so Chambers proclaimed that Prince Fred would take his place alongside the heroes of antiquity. And by the same token, his own design was worthy of joining the ruins of Rome.

When Chambers returned to Britain an important early patron was Frederick's widow, Princess Augusta, whose gardens at Kew were later to become the Botanical Gardens. He embellished Kew with ornamental follies, of which the pagoda is the most celebrated. They included an archway built as a viaduct to carry people and cattle over the princess's private footpath; built in 1759, this was perhaps the earliest artificial ruin to be built in the classical style in Britain. In Chambers's own words:

> My intention was to imitate Roman antiquity, built of brick, with an incrustation of stone . . . The north front is confined between rocks, overgrown with briars and other wild plants, and topped with thickets, amongst which are seen several columns, and other fragments of buildings, and at a little distance beyond the arch is seen an antique statue of a Muse.

The arch survives today but is bald of these charms, with the Muse under lock and key in a museum. Fortunately, the scented glade of Chambers's imagination is preserved in a painting by Richard Wilson, an artist best known for his views of Italian landscapes. Wilson abetted his friend's deception: in the canvas the sky has a Mediterranean luminosity, and a Grand Tourist sketches in the shadow of a

*The Ruined Arch in Kew Gardens* by Richard Wilson, *c.*1761–2.
This arch in imitation of the 'Roman antiquity' was a viaduct in the
private estate of Augusta, widow of the Prince of Wales. It still
stands in the Botanical Gardens.

cypress. Indeed, until 1948 the painting was thought to be
a view taken in the Borghese Gardens.

But Chambers's most ironic illustration is a design for the
interior of a villa at Roehampton, seen in a drawing which is
now in the Victoria and Albert Museum. Parksted was built
for the Earl of Bessborough and intended to be glimpsed
across Richmond Park as if it were an antique temple in a
grove of trees. A basement room displayed Bessborough's
collection of china, and its vaulted ceiling was to be painted
with a *trompe-l'oeil* pergola, a design based on the
decoration of a Roman tomb. But there was a second level
of *trompe-l'oeil*: the design drawing was itself an illusion,

pretending to be a piece of paper which had been ripped in two. The device flattered Bessborough's recollections of his own Grand Tour to Italy: fingering the drawing he must have felt that he was recovering some fragment of antiquity.

What could be more 'postmodernist' than this drawing? If Sterne's *Tristam Shandy* prefigures the postmodernist novel, then Chambers's drawings predate every ironic trick in American postmodernist architecture of the 1990s – except one: Wonderworks in Orlando, Florida. This Museum of Natural Phenomena was designed by architect Terry Nicholson to resemble a courthouse from the Bahamas which has been picked up by a hurricane and dropped, upside-down, on to a citrus-packing warehouse in downtown Orlando. Designed in the neo-Palladian colonial

Wonderworks: The Museum of Natural Phenomena, in Orlando, Florida.

style, the courthouse is literally upside-down, with palm-trees dangling from the sky. The pediment shatters the pavement like a meteorite and visitors enter through a fissure in the masonry to stroll over the ceilings. The Rev. William Gilpin had declared in one of his Picturesque guidebooks of the 1770s that a country house in the symmetrical, boxy Palladian style could only be transformed into a Picturesque object by seizing a mallet and battering one half into a pile of rubble. He had never seen a hurricane.

In the eighteenth century the boldest experiments with classical ruins were in Germany, where the rulers of rival principalities competed in lavishness in the design of palaces, churches, gardens and garden follies. In 1730 Prince-Bishop Damian Hugo von Schonborn of Speyer built a hermitage in the garden of his palace at Waghausel in the form of a dilapidated wooden roof on stone columns, the ceiling painted in 'hermit fashion' in the manner of Clérisseau's ruin room. At Bayreuth the Margrave of Brandenburg-Bayreuth created a series of cells in the woods in which members of the court would live the lives of Carthusian monks. In 1735 he gave the gardens to his wife Wilhelmine, who added a ruinous amphitheatre for the performance of open-air opera. She was the sister of Frederick the Great, who created the remarkable *ruinenberg* at his palace of Sanssouci in 1748. The summit of a hill was levelled to form a shallow circular amphitheatre, across which a triple-storeyed arcade of the Colosseum faced a circular Doric temple, a row of Ionic columns and a rugged obelisk.

An extravagant response to Gilpin's suggestion of how to transform Palladian formality into Picturesque disorder was a design commissioned in 1791 by Prince Wilhelm I of

Hesse-Kassel, imagining the transformation of the central block of his newly built neo-classical Schloss Wilhelmslöhe into a romantic ruin. Was this just a visual amusement, or did the fantasy of demolishing portico, staircase and halls of state indicate some desperate desire to escape the duty of government? The design remained on paper, but the prince commissioned the same architect to build a ruinous mock-medieval castle in the depths of his hunting park. The crumbling curtain walls of Schloss Löwenburg suggested that the castle had been abandoned, but concealed behind the parapets was a suite of apartments decorated in a style that appealed to the prince's fantasy of himself as a knight of the Middle Ages. This was his private love nest, where he and his favourite mistress escaped the ceremony of court. The Löwenburg is a happy echo of Henry II and Rosamund Clifford at Woodstock, and also the perfect illustration of how a garden ruin played the role of *alter ego* to the palace of state in the principalities of eighteenth-century Germany.

The most magical artificial ruin in eighteenth-century Europe was the theatre built in the garden of the Lazienski Palace in Warsaw by Stanislaus Augustus, the King of Poland. Beside the lake was a semicircular amphitheatre with twenty tiers of seating. The stage was on the island, and encircled by trees so that the idyllic scene of antiquity was invisible to anyone but the theatre audience. The design of the proscenium was based upon that excavated at Herculaneum, and a bricolage of Corinthian columns receded into the woodland. The theatre was inaugurated in 1791 with a performance of the ballet *Cleopatra*, no doubt chosen to suit the scenery. With lamps suspended from the trees, and the dancers in their robes ferried to the island, the scene must have been as seductive as a tableau painted by Claude or Watteau. That evening was a blissful climax to the cult of the ruin in eighteenth-century Europe.

Stanislaus Augustus believed that art could create an identity for his troubled nation, but two years later Poland was invaded by Russia and Prussia, partitioned, and wiped from the map of Europe. The last King of Poland died in exile in St Petersburg, and his people endured two decades of bloodshed caused by revolution and foreign wars. In the years which followed, how many of the audience wished that – like sailors swimming to join the mermaids – they had crossed the water and entered forever the magical illusion of Arcadia?

There was a tragic finale to the cult of the ruin in France also. Gardens in the Picturesque, English style had become a fashionable mania in the two decades before the Revolution of 1789, and their folly-ruins came to symbolise, in turn, the decadence of the rulers, the failed hopes of the Enlightenment philosophers, and the brutality of the Revolutionaries. The flakiness of the *ancien régime* was exemplified by the gâteaux in the form of classical ruins which were served to the royal family by the great chef Antoine Carême, or by the Picturesque imitation farm which was created for Marie-Antoinette beside a lake in the grounds of Versailles. When she and her ladies-in-waiting grew bored of the ritual of court they played at being shepherdesses in an idle mockery of the toils of agricultural life. Aristocrats and financiers joined the royal family in lavishing fortunes on creating *jardins anglais* at their châteaux around Paris. The Comte d'Albion married a financier's daughter and built such a full catalogue of follies

Design by Antoine Carême for a cake served to the French royal family. Carême's interest in architecture was such that he presented a plan for the reconstruction of St Petersburg to Czar Alexander I.

at his château of Franconville that in three years he was bankrupt and divorced: a Temple of the Muses, a hermitage, funerary monuments, a Devil's Bridge, a column in honour of Mirabeau, a grotto dedicated to Edward Young (the author of *Night Thoughts*), the god Pan, two rustic huts, a windmill, a pond and a fisherman's house, a shepherd's hut, an obelisk, a pyramid, and an island dedicated to a Dutch doctor named Boerhave.

The French were fonder of philosophical inscriptions than the English. The most philosophical of gardens was Ermenonville where the Marquis de Girardin threw down the walls of his rectangular, formal garden and erected more

than fifty symbolic follies in Arcadian countryside. Girardin
had toured English gardens but he was also a disciple of
Rousseau, devoutly following his belief in the instinctive
goodness of Nature. He raised his children according to the
lessons of the novel *Emile*, and built a replica of the
philosopher's mountain hut. Rousseau died in Girardin's
care in 1778, and was buried at Ermenonville in a neo-
Roman sarcophagus on an island of poplars. He was the first
man to be buried in a garden since antiquity, but so popular
did this cult become that the garden soon became an Elysian
Fields of sarcophagi. There is even the tomb of a deranged
English disciple who swam across to Rousseau's grave and
there blew his brains out.

On the hill overlooking the lake stood a circular temple
which at first sight appeared to be a ruin but was, in fact,
only half-built. The 'Temple of Philosophy' had the names
of six thinkers inscribed on its six columns – Newton,
Descartes, William Penn, Montesquieu, Rousseau and
Voltaire – and symbolised the Marquis's hope that the
Enlightenment was a work-in-progress, its topping-out still
to come. The scene of lake, sarcophagus, poplars and temple
was created by the landscape painter Hubert Robert, who
was perhaps the principal figure in the Picturesque taste of
the court. According to a friend, Robert was 'neither an
architect, nor a gardener, he is a poet and a painter, who
composes landscapes'. 'Robert (Hubert) called Robert des
Ruines, painter' was written on his death certificate in 1808.
His career during the Revolution shows the cruel final twist
in the tale of the Picturesque – and how by dramatic irony
the unfinished Temple of Philosophy became a real ruin.

Robert had arrived as an art student in Rome in 1754, at

the age of twenty-one, and remained there for eleven years for, as he wrote on one drawing, ROMA QUANTA FUIT / IPSA RUINA DOCET. ('The ruins themselves teach us how great Rome was.') When he and his friend Fragonard made an excursion to Hadrian's villa at Tivoli they scratched their names into the plasterwork, as Chateaubriand had seen, and the sketches they made in crayon are some of the most exquisite drawings of ruins ever committed to paper. On his return to France he exhibited the first of hundreds of ruinscapes at the Paris Salon in 1767 and was hailed by Denis Diderot as a new voice of *vanitas.* 'The ideas aroused within me by ruins are lofty', wrote Diderot in his review of the exhibition. 'Everything vanishes, everything perishes, everything passes away; the world alone remains, time alone continues. How old this world is! I walk between these two eternities. . . . What is my ephemeral existence compared to that of this crumbling stone?'

The philosopher was soon disillusioned by his protégé's liveliness: 'He wants to earn ten *louis* in a morning; he is lavish, his wife is chic.' In a succession of canvases his contemporaries saw the Temple of Vesta at Tivoli, the Roman structure which was the model for the Temple of Philosophy at Ermenonville, change its form in a blur of inventive variations: the circular structure was domed, thatched, then open to the sky; its columns were Doric, Ionic and Corinthian; it was placed on a cliff or a lake, and then became a hovel for beggars, a refuge for bandits, a windmill, and the bubbling source of a spring at which peasants wash their rags. . . . Robert painted with astonishing rapidity and facility. He was a warm-hearted and lovable man, who never shared Diderot's interest in the

metaphysical meaning of ruins. To him, the depiction of
mouldering grandeur was a means to pay for a new silk dress
for his wife for that evening's ball.

It required a revolution to introduce dark undertones to
Robert's ruins. Robert was imprisoned in the Terror,
implicated by the presence of his pictures in every salon of
the *ancien régime*. Even in gaol he painted and painted,
alternating between sombre studies of prisoners condemned
to the guillotine and escapist fantasies of Arcadia. Materials
were short, and still surviving in the Musée Carnavalet are
several examples of prison crockery painted with ruins,
waterfalls and shepherds. When he was released in July
1794, he found that Paris was suddenly littered with brand-
new ruins of palaces and churches plundered and des-
ecrated. The Russian envoy noted the irony in a letter to
Catherine the Great: 'One must presume that Robert must
find himself like a *coq en pâte* [in clover]. . . . On each side
that he turns he finds his genre supreme, and the most
beautiful and the most fresh ruins in the world.' However,
Robert's priority was to paint the heroic events of the
Revolution in order to win favour with the regime: he
recorded the Bastille being demolished; the coffins of the
French kings being exhumed from the crypt of the Abbey of
Saint-Denis in order to celebrate the first anniversary of
the abolition of monarchy; the ceremonial procession of
the urn containing Rousseau's ashes from the garden at
Ermenonville to the new, secular temple of the Pantheon
in Paris. He succeeded, and a year after his release was
appointed to the Committee superintending the conversion
of this royal palace into a museum showing the royal
collection of art and antiquities. It is impossible to know the

true feelings of this old and impoverished man whose world had been turned upside down, and it is only the famous view of the *Louvre in Ruins* which gives us an inkling of his inner confusion. At the Paris Salon of 1796 Robert exhibited a design showing the remodelling of the Grand Galerie which runs parallel to the banks of the Seine into a top-lit picture gallery of apparently endless length. Its pendant projected the same view in ruins. An artist is drawing the statue of Apollo while peasants burn picture-frames for fuel. Every detail of this composition – the vault in fragments, the vegetation, artists sharing the ruin with peasants – was

*Imaginary View of the Grand Galerie of the Louvre in Ruins* by Hubert Robert, 1796. This futuristic view is the first example of an artist imagining how an existing structure might appear after a future cataclysm.

transferred from his Roman scenes in order to represent the future of Paris. In the rubble were three masterpieces, each intact: the Apollo Belvedere, with the bust of Raphael at its feet, and a 'Slave' by Michelangelo. In times of turmoil the immortality of art seemed the only certainty.

Robert was the first artist to paint an existing building in ruins. This unprecedented image may have been influenced by the Comte de Volney's *Les Ruines, ou Méditation sur les révolutions des empires*, published in Paris in 1791. Volney was a deputy in the National Assembly that had been formed

Frontispiece to *Les Ruines* by the Comte de Volney (1791), engraved by Martini.

in 1789, and a leading intellectual light of the Revolution. As a young traveller he had written the archaeological study *Voyage en Syrie* and he began *Les Ruines* by recalling a solitary evening in the magnificent desolation of Palmyra: '*Je vous salue, ruines solitaires, tombeaux saints, murs silencieux!*' Seated on a hillside, he surveyed the vast ruins on the valley floor and imagined Palmyra in its prime as the great entrepôt of desert traders during the Roman Empire. 'Where are they now, the ramparts of Nineveh, the walls of Babylon, the fleets of Tyre?' And what will happen on the 'banks of the Seine, of the Thames, of the Zyder-zee'? His soliloquy on the cruelty of Time and the inevitability of ruin is silenced by a genie who appears from the ruins and commands an end to such sentimental clichés. Ruin is not an inevitable cycle in Nature, the spirit explains, nor is it a law of God. Ruin is the consequence of human pride, greed and stupidity. It was not Nature or God or Time which laid waste to Palmyra but man, and man alone. The genie whirls Volney high into the sky to show him how the surface of the globe is scarred by war, plunder and exploitation. The French Revolution is the opportunity for the enlightenment of mankind and its creation of a universal, prosperous peace. Volney's epiphany in Palmyra was a prologue to his manifesto for a 'general assembly of the nations' governed by 'a pyramid of natural law'. Whatever his views on Volney's political agenda, Robert's fantasy of the Louvre might have been suggested by the writer's image of ruins on the banks of the River Seine.

The cruellest inversion of the *ancien régime*'s pleasure in follies was *Le Jardin Elysée des Monuments Français*, a subject Robert painted four times. This was an assemblage of funerary monuments salvaged by Alexandre Lenoir from churches and châteaux after their vandalisation by the Revolutionaries and placed inside the cloisters and gardens of the redundant convent of the Petits-Augustins. They included the tombs from the abbey of Saint-Denis, where the French kings had been buried since the Middle Ages. Lenoir placed the monuments between trees in the style of Ermenonville, intending the effect of '*la douce mélancolie qui parle à l'âme sensible*' ('the sweet melancholy which speaks to the sensitive soul'). In the manner of a capriccio by Clérisseau – or of William Stukeley's garden hermitage – each of the monuments in the Elysian garden was, in fact, a Picturesque assembly of fragments from various sources. But all the charms of eighteenth-century taste could not obscure the tragic implications of ruins. Indeed, the Royalist Chateaubriand was later to write: 'I cannot better depict society in 1789 and 1790 than by likening it to the collection of ruins and tombs of all ages heaped pell-mell, after the Terror, in the cloisters of the Petits-Augustins.'

In 1818 a *divorcée* named Mme Hugo came to live in an apartment on the third floor of No. 18 rue des Petits-Augustins, a house created inside the shell of the convent. Her son Victor was eighteen years old, and already displaying a precocious brilliance as a poet. Although he was to die the hero of Europe's workers, the young Victor Hugo was a fervent and vocal supporter of the restored Bourbons. His brother Abel was also a Royalist, and published his political theories in a book named *Les Tombeaux de Saint-Denis*, its central image the cruel Elysium visible from their windows.

An elderly visitor who frequently climbed the stairs of No.

18 was a cousin of Mme Hugo, the Comte de Volney. Two decades of bloodshed, destruction and darkness had followed the bright new dawn in which he wrote his *Les Ruines.* As he had once looked down on Palmyra, now he looked down on this silent garden of ruins with the young Victor Hugo at his side. What did Volney's genie say now? Perhaps Hugo's poem, 'Before the Arc de Triomphe' is a last echo of that evening in Palmyra. It is a vision of Paris in years to come:

> When the banks where the water breaks on sonorous
> bridges
> Are covered once again with the murmuring reeds . . .
> When the Seine flows on over obstacles of stone
> Eroding some old dome which has tumbled into its
> stream . . .

# VIII
# Self-portrait in Ruins

Leptis Magna is not the only imported Roman ruin in Britain. In London, the catacombs of Sir John Soane's Museum display statues, altars and fragments of architecture, piled in the shadows as if they had been excavated hours before. Light trickles into the subterranean labyrinth from skylights high above; there are no windows, so there are no views of the modern city outside. As soon as the front door closes the visitor is no longer in central London but, rather, inside the imaginative world of the museum's founder. The great architect died in this house at No. 13 Lincoln's Inn Fields in 1837, and the interiors have not been altered since. The museum was created as a form of autobiography, and its collection has been described as 'treasures salvaged from a shipwrecked dream'. I worked there for five years, and it required five years to begin to understand John Soane's obsession with ruin. Few architects have better understood the illusions and ironies of their medium. And no man has ever been more distrustful of posterity than Soane.

Born the youngest son of a bricklayer in 1753, Soane rose to rival John Nash as the most successful architect of Regency London. He was an architect of genius who designed some of the most beautiful interiors in Britain, and in his professional practice he was punctilious, efficient and worldly. In his private life, however, he was introspective, melancholy and quarrelsome. Soane was the first architect to bring to the world of bricks, mortar and property development the *Sturm und Drang* of the Romantic movement, as personified by the painters Henry Fuseli and Benjamin Robert Haydon. Inspired by Rousseau and by Goethe's *Young Werther*, this generation of artists of the 1780s invented the idea that creative genius was identified with uncompromising self-expression – and that the consequence of the refusal to compromise was misunderstanding, persecution and failure. In the painter's garret this idea had its charm, but Soane was architect to the Directors of the Bank of England, the Lord Chancellor and the Prime Minister. He had to hang his Romantic cloak in a cupboard.

The tensions between these two sides of his personality were expressed through the metaphor of ruin. This first appeared when in 1795 he rebuilt the Stock Exchange, which was then a circular domed hall within the Bank of England complex. He celebrated its completion by commissioning a painting from Joseph Gandy, a young architect who had been studying in Rome until Napoleon invaded. Gandy immediately demonstrated a genius for painting perspective representations of his master's designs, and remained Soane's visualising amanuensis for the next thirty years. Each year the paintings were exhibited at the Royal Academy's annual exhibition.

The week after Gandy painted the Rotunda intact, he presented Soane with a second painting in which he imagined the same structure in ruins. The City of London is suddenly a wilderness, a desolate landscape as *disabitato* as Rome in the Dark Ages. The caryatids which supported the

*View of the Rotunda of the Bank of England in Ruins* by Joseph Gandy, 1798. John Soane's assistant, Gandy, imagined the Bank of England when London was a wasteland.

lid of Soane's dome are silhouetted against a menacing sky, silently watching the *calciatori* who are pillaging marble to burn into lime. Soane's Bank was demolished in 1925 and photographs in *The Times* have an uncanny similarity to Gandy's vision, even down to the demolition men swinging their pickaxes. As ever, posterity is a dab hand at dramatic irony.

But why was the painting made? It was not exhibited at the Royal Academy until Soane retired more than three decades later. It might have been motivated by the public criticisms of the design of the new Rotunda; certainly, ruins came to express the architect's sense of persecution. An anonymous poem called 'The Modern Goth' ridiculing the design of the Stock Exchange was read aloud to great

Gandy's prophesy came true when the Bank was demolished in 1925, as pictured by *The Times* on 1st May.

hilarity at a dinner of the Architects' Club held in Soane's absence: his innovation of decorating a surface with incised patterns of abstract lines, for example, was described as 'pilasters scored like loins of pork'. Soane sued for libel, unsuccessfully. In his *Memoirs* he presented the episode as evidence of how 'a *corps collectif* was organised against me', a group which – so he claimed – continued to persecute him until the end of his life. Soane was the first British architect to insist upon a recognisable, personal style of design, what journalists call 'signature architecture' today. It was not an issue of marketing in Soane's case, however, but the Romantics' belief in individual self-expression.

The artist Gandy shared Soane's visionary approach to architecture, and also his refusal to compromise. Yet he lacked his master's ability with clients and lived and died in graceless penury, often relying on hand-outs from Soane in order to feed his children. As Soane grew older, he commissioned Gandy to paint increasingly fantastic visions of London as a 'new Rome' with a procession of arches, columns and palaces advancing from Kensington Gore to Whitehall. It is almost as if Gandy was an expression of one side of Soane's personality: like Dorian Gray's portrait in the attic, he was nurtured and fed in order to keep alive the patron's ideal of his profession.

In 1830 Gandy painted one of the finest architectural drawings ever made in Britain, a bird's-eye view of the entire complex of the Bank of England in ruins. The drawing celebrated Soane's completion of the complex after forty-five years as an architect, in which time the Bank had become a city in itself with a fortified perimeter wall pierced by gateways designed in the form of triumphal arches. Now he retired, telling the Directors that the project was 'the pride and the boast of my life'.

But why present his life's work as a ruin? It is a puzzle. First, is this indeed a ruin? It might be seen as a type of drawing called 'a cutaway axonometric', a device to lift the lid of a building and expose the ingenuity of its ground-plan and the quality of its construction. In the words of Daniel Abramson, 'a combination of plan, section and elevation – the totality of Soane's achievement is represented: interior and exterior, construction and decoration, substructure and superstructure, all publicly revealed like a model on a table-top'. Soane was particularly proud of the mighty stone walls, designed to resist the assaults of French soldiers or British revolutionaries. As a lecturer on architecture said at the time, the Bank was 'massive and noble, its construction of genuine brick, iron and stone. When London is fallen ("and such as Memphis is, London shall be!", *Old Play*) this building along with those of Wren, and the bridges, will be almost the only ruins left to indicate its present greatness.' Peering closely at the drawing, we see that its mood is very different from the earlier view of the Rotunda: each column is upright, no stone is mouldering, and except for the trees in the Governor's Garden there is not a whisper of menacing vegetation. The site is as pristine as a desert excavation. If the ruins of London were to be uncovered by archaeologists of the future the flimsy brick-and-stucco terraces flung up in Regent's Park by his rival John Nash would have disappeared into oblivion, but the remains of the Bank would be as impressive as those of classical antiquity.

In addition to commissioning these fantasies, Soane also built two artificial ruins: Gothic in Lincoln's Inn Fields, classical at his country house in Ealing, Pitshanger Manor. When he was forty-seven years old he built Pitshanger as a country refuge for the family. The choice was a deliberate act of autobiography, however: his first job in the architect's office had been to assist in the erection of a new wing at the old manor house, and this extension was the only block he did not demolish after buying the estate. Two years later, in 1802, he announced to the press: 'There has lately been discovered in the manor of Pitshanger at Ealing the remains of a very ancient Temple, which for the satisfaction of all lovers of antiquity I shall describe': the ruins of a colonnaded structure behind the kitchens, with an altar that

View by George Basevi, one of Soane's pupils, of the ruins at Pitshanger Manor, 1810. At his country house in Ealing, Soane created a classical ruin which he pretended was a Roman temple discovered while constructing the kitchen block, visible at the left.

suggested the site of a Roman temple, and 'in clearing away a part of the ground a large Horn was discovered which makes me conclude the Temple was consecrated to Jupiter Ammon'.

The ruin was, of course, a hoax, and this manuscript a pastiche of the type of article which antiquarians regularly contributed to the *Gentleman's Magazine*. A semicircular colonnade and a sunken archway faced the back wall of the kitchen, in the centre of which was a blocked doorway flanked by fluted Corinthian columns. These forms were couplets and quatrains of classical architecture, quotations fractured from the original text, as in Wyattville's folly at Virginia Water. And like Wyattville, Soane depended upon his audience's imagining that the site had been submerged by the debris of previous centuries. But that by itself was too simple for Soane. If the doorway rested upon the ground, why were the columns buried so deeply? His trick was to choose as his model the temple at the sacred spring of Clitumnus, near Spoleto, exceptional in Roman architecture as having a doorway at first-floor level, leading to a balcony from which 'Priests or Magi delivered their exhortations or oracles to the people below'. The buried columns were therefore the ground floor, and the doorway the balcony above.

These 'finds' were presented to friends who came for the three days of Ealing's summer fair in 1804, and who were invited to suggest their own reconstructions of the tumbled fragments hidden under brambles. It was a parlour game, and Soane later admitted that 'one of my objects was to ridicule those fanciful architects and antiquarians who, finding a few pieces of columns, and sometimes only a few single stones, proceeded from these slender data to imagine magnificent buildings'. But what was built as a *jeu d'esprit* in the prime of life acquired a sinister aspect in his old age. He had hoped that the environment he created at Pitshanger would inspire his teenage sons to become architects and that John, the elder of the two, would be the first of a dynasty of Soanes to reside there. But after ten years he accepted defeat and sold the estate. John Jr did train as an architect but was idle and passionless, and did very little with his life before succumbing to tuberculosis in 1823. Happening to pass through Ealing shortly afterwards, Soane took the opportunity to revisit Pitshanger. 'Oh John, John, what has idleness cost you!' he wrote in his diary that evening. In hindsight, his disappointment focused on the ruin. When John was an undergraduate at Cambridge 'I recommended

to him to restore the ruins of Pitshanger, an idea with which
he expressed great satisfaction, and I flattered myself that on
his return from college I should have seen his sketches and
ideas on the subject. In this I was disappointed.' The non-
appearance of the drawings was the first indication of the
tepidness of his son's enthusiasm for architecture. We can
only speculate on the psychological implications of the
exercise: a puzzle whose only correct solution is locked
inside his father's mind.

The new owner of Pitshanger demolished the ruins and
built a coal-store in their place. In a final codicil to the story,
two years before his death in 1837 Soane published a
volume of views of the estate in which he pretended that the
site had been excavated to reveal a mosaic pavement and
battered statues. The disappearance of the folly enabled him
to embellish what had actually existed behind the kitchens,
adding columns, urns and sculptured bas-reliefs. These
additions were copied from the façade of the house itself,
tempting us to wonder if he is visualising his former home
as a ruin. Soane had designed its façade to be 'a picture, a
sort of self-portrait' of an architect and connoisseur at the
height of his success. Are these views made thirty years later
a self-portrait in ruins?

The second artificial ruin Soane built survives in a
courtyard at the rear of the museum at Lincoln's Inn Fields.
The 'Monk's Yard' is one of the oddest spots in London, a
Gothic cloister and tomb which connect to the Monk's
Parlour and Cell, two small rooms illuminated by stained
glass and decorated with Gothic souvenirs. The sequence of
spaces has been described by Helen Dorey, the historian of
the Museum, as a 'Gothic novel in miniature'. In the guide-

book he wrote Soane pretended that he had discovered the remains when digging the foundations of his new house: in medieval times, he explained, this had been the hermitage of a monk named Padre Giovanni. In fact, he had assembled the ruin from pieces he had salvaged in his role as architect to the old Houses of Parliament, once the medieval Palace of Westminster, which was subsequently destroyed by fire. The arches of the cloister were thirteenth-century window-frames from the House of Lords, while a projecting canopy once sheltered a statue in its niche on the façade of Westminster Hall. Although the ruin was built in 1824, Soane continued the Picturesque tradition of the eighteenth century in knocking together the fragments of various centuries in order to create a stage-set; indeed, he had visited Lenoir's Jardin Elysée in Paris. The tomb itself is inscribed *Alas Poor Fanny!*, as if Padre Giovanni had withdrawn into seclusion because of a broken heart. But Fanny was Mrs Soane's beloved pet dog, and its tiny coffin still lies in the Monk's Grave. Soane was satirising the contemporary hysteria for the Gothic, as Jane Austen had done in *Northanger Abbey*. But he was also concealing a genuine sadness. Soane's beloved wife Eliza had died two years after he built the house, and he lived alone for the last two decades of his life. Padre Giovanni is 'Father John', and the hermit in his cell became an *alter ego* of the lonely old architect.

Soane's most astonishing image of ruin is in a manuscript he wrote entitled 'Crude Hints Towards the History of My House', in which he imagines an antiquarian of the future picking over its ruins. 'Crude Hints' was never published, and has been described as the oddest document in the history of architecture. The manuscript ends in a splutter of exclamation marks, and is inscribed with three dates – 30 August, 7 September and 22 September: it was written in three spurts of rage during the summer of 1812 when his new house at No. 13 Lincoln's Inn Fields was under construction.

Soane imagines that after his death his house is occupied by lawyers, and then falls into disuse. It is supposed to be haunted, and for several centuries no one enters, until a curious antiquarian pushes open the door. The pieces of Soane's collection were a trail of clues as to the purpose of the building. 'A Votive hand and foot indicate this building to have been a temple – and the *cornu ammonis* designates it as dedicated to Jupiter', the archaeologist writes on discovering the statue of the god Jupiter and the horn-shaped fossil which still stand in one of the courtyards of the museum today. However:

> The Columns describe a Colonnade of a kind almost
> peculiar to Convents, and as these Columns are of the
> Ionic or feminine order it is reasonable to conclude
> from thence that it had been a convent of Nuns, & not
> a Heathen Temple. The Sphinx, The Griffon & Lamb
> carry us very far back into Antiquity – & the flat vaulted
> Ceiling of the great Crypt is in itself so truly Egyptian
> that –

A halt; the exploration is erratic. Soon the antiquarian is wondering whether it might have been 'the residence of a magician', and if a prominent statue is 'this very necromancer turned into marble' as a punishment for his audacity. There is no staircase, and peering into the black depths of the well he wonders if this is where Vestal Virgins were buried alive.

There was no staircase when Soane wrote, because No. 13 was under construction. Half-built became half-ruined in his eyes as a consequence of a series of events that summer which caused his persecution complex to return. The first hint as to what really happened is when the antiquarian relates a legend of how the design of the façade caused such offence to 'lovers of pure architecture' that 'an officer yclept the district Surveyor . . . boldly entered his veto against this particular work'. Soane is referring to what we call a planning dispute today. Two weeks before he began writing, the district surveyor had knocked on the door and instructed him to demolish the stone verandah which projected 3 feet 6 inches beyond the building line specified by the Building Acts. Soane refused, and took his case to the High Court. He won, but simultaneously he was suspended from his post of Lecturer in Architecture at the Royal Academy. He had attacked a rival's design for the new opera house in Covent Garden, and it was against the rules to criticise a fellow Academician in a lecture. Soane's sense of isolation was reflected in the fictional antiquarian's conclusion: the ruin in Lincoln's Inn Fields was not a temple, convent, or magician's lair but the home of a persecuted artist, who 'from a pure love to promote the interests of Art . . . raised a nest of wasps about him sufficient to sting the strongest man to death'. Did he ever – wonders Helen Dorey, who has transcribed the manuscript – picture himself buried alive in the basement catacombs? Soane finished his first draft as follows:

he saw the views of early youth blighted – his fairest
prospects utterly destroyed – his lively character became
sombre – melancholy, brooding constantly over an
accumulation of evils brought him into a state little
short of mental derangement, his enemies perceived this
– they seized the moment – they smote his rock & he
fell as many had done before him and died as was
generally believed of a broken heart.

But why 'a broken heart'? In the last version the ending
placed more emphasis on the failures of his children:

What an admirable picture to show the vanity &
mockery of all human expectations – the man who
founded this place fondly imagined that the children of
his children would have inhabited the place for Ages &
that he had laid the foundation of an establishment
which would daily gain strength and produce a race of
Artists that would have done honour to their Country –
Oh what a falling off do these ruins present – the
subject becomes too gloomy to be pursued – the pen
drops from my almost palsied hand.

The broken heart was caused by his younger son George,
whose delinquency coincided with the disputes at the High
Court and the Royal Academy. George had more spark
than his brother John, but refused to become an architect.
Determined to be a playwright, he had joined Bohemian
society and was continually pestering his parents for money.
On the third occasion Soane refused and George was
consigned to the debtors' prison. He never forgave his

father and three years later, in 1815, penned two
anonymous attacks on 'Soanean' architecture in a London
newspaper named *The Champion*. Eliza Soane was ill when
she read the article but rose to exclaim, 'This is George's
doing. I can never hold up my head again. He has given me
my death blow.' Six weeks later she died, and afterwards
George was exposed as the author. Soane pasted the
*Champion* articles on to a blackboard which he placed on
display in the house. Its label was a piece of wood as heavy
as the proverbial blunt instrument, inscribed with the words
*Death Blows Given by George Soane*.

Father and son did not speak again, and the quarrel cast a
shadow over the remaining twenty-two years of Sir John
Soane's life in Lincoln's Inn Fields. At the age of eighty, in
1833, he gave his house and its collection to the government by an Act of Parliament. One clause specified that the
curator 'shall keep it as nearly as possible in the state in
which Sir John Soane shall leave it'. His chair has not moved
from the fireside, and the clock still ticks on the mantelpiece,
as if your host has just stepped out for a moment. Indeed,
Soane opened his house to the public on Sundays and it is
not too fanciful to imagine him concealed in the shadows
and listening to the whispered speculations of visitors; it was
his chance to eavesdrop on the judgement of posterity. The
museum remained closed, however, on 'wet or gloomy'
days: its magic depended upon a blue, Mediterranean sky.

The moment the Act became law Soane placed a marble
bust of himself in the Dome of the museum. The image – as
imperious as Caesar, promised the sculptor – commanded
centre stage, asserting the permanency of his bequest.
However, the fragments of classical architecture and

Soane's bust presides over a scene of suspended ruin displayed in the domed space at the centre of his museum at No. 13 Lincoln's Inn Fields.

Like Soane at Agrigento, many young architects have measured themselves against the giants of the classical world. This photograph of Le Corbusier (Charles Edward Jeanneret) in the Acropolis, studying a fluted column, was taken by his friend Klipstein in 1911.

sculpture surrounding the bust give the irresistible sensation of imminent ruin – or ruin perhaps momentarily suspended. The contrast between fragility and permanence illustrated the unresolved dialogue in the founder's mind: having no deep religious conviction, he based his hopes of immortality on architecture. And yet, architecture was so flimsy . . .

My mind always returns to an image in the lectures he gave to the students at the Royal Academy, when he analysed the Greek temple of Jupiter Olympian at Agrigento in Sicily. Its Doric columns were the second biggest in all antiquity and by way of illustrating their vast girth, Soane described how a man could lie inside one of their grooves. He had arrived in Agrigento in the winter of 1779, a scholarship student travelling with three close friends. It was perhaps the happiest time of his life. Tired of wandering through the columns which lie scattered in the dust like giant, chopped celery, the tall, skinny youth stretched out inside a flute to rest. For the next fifty years his life was a heroic struggle to measure himself against the grandeur of antiquity.

# IX

# The Ozymandias Complex

To the Royal Academy audience in 1830, Soane's picture of the Bank of England in ruins was a prophecy of the end of London. For, as we have seen, travellers to the ruins of antiquity were not only contemplating past greatness but also considering the future of their own societies. Babylon and Memphis, Mycenae and Troy, Athens, Carthage and Rome: why not London?

Soane's view of the Bank shared the walls of the Royal Academy exhibition with a multiplicity of designs by architects proposing the reconstruction of London as a city as magnificent as ancient Rome. Neo-classical splendour befitted a city which was the richest and largest in the world, the capital of a nation which had been victorious at Waterloo in 1815. It was in the years after the defeat of Napoleon that Nelson's Column was erected in Trafalgar Square, triumphal arches rose on Constitution Hill, and a colossal bronze of Wellington in the guise of a naked classical warrior was erected in Hyde Park. The wealth of this new Empire flowed from trade and navigation: the Bank of England and Royal Exchange were as monumental in their design as the Roman Forum, and in many of the architects' designs we see merchantmen unloading the tribute of the globe on quays ornamented with marble colonnades, bronze statues and mighty flights of steps. In *The Golden Bowl* (1904) Henry

James's Prince Amerigo reflected that window-shopping on Bond Street brought him closer to the reality of his native city in the days of its imperial splendour than any archaeological textbook, and standing on London Bridge to watch the ships pass by the Thames seemed to be a modern incarnation of the Tiber. But it was on a broken arch of London Bridge that we met the New Zealander, the harbinger of a future doom. As self-identification with the virtues of an ancient Empire increased in strength, so did doubts as to whether its vices would lead to decline and fall.

In Lincoln's Inn Fields, beside the view of the Stock

*The Fall of Babylon* by John Martin, painted in 1819 and published as an engraving twelve years later. This awe-inspiring visualisation of Biblical destruction attracted an audience of thousands when it was exhibited in London in 1819 – and paid off the artist's debts.

Exchange in ruins, Soane hung a lithograph of John Martin's *Fall of Babylon*, painted in 1819. At the exhibition that year the painter sold £1,000-worth of tickets in four days, as a crowd jostled in front of the 7 × 11 feet canvas which depicted the cursed city falling to the armies of Cyrus the Great in 538 BC. Elbowing their way to the rope, they could enjoy the anecdotal details of King Belshazzar surrounded by his concubines, the elephants of Cyrus bellowing in the streets, and the Tower of Babel behind the stormy clouds. Martin prided himself on the accuracy of his reconstructions, combining biblical texts and recent surveys in the desert, and never declared any intention to compare London to Babylon. His audience had no doubts, however, and in *The Last Judgement* of 1857 the artist admitted as much by showing a steam train with top-hatted passengers hurtling into God's gulf of fire.

Martin's younger brother Jonathan made the analogy explicit. He was an insane religious fanatic who set fire to York Minster as a warning to the bishops of the Church of England of their impending destruction. 'You blind Hypocrites, you serpents and vipers of Hell, you wine bibbers and beef eaters, whose eyes stand out with fatness', he wrote in a letter of 16 January 1832. He was incarcerated in Bedlam until his death six years later and there he scrawled an astonishing adaptation of one of his brother's prints. The scene is retitled *London's Sad Overthrow* and we see Westminster Abbey and St Paul's in flames on the horizon as the city is invaded by French armies, Napoleon on a white horse replacing Cyrus on an elephant. A lion is in the sky, and bishops carouse in the foreground. On the reverse are his precise calculations of the debts owed to him

*London's Overthrow* by Jonathan Martin, 1832. Jonathan was a religious fanatic who redrew his elder brother's visions of religious cataclysm to show God's divine vengeance on a corrupt London.

by the government, and an addled rant based upon Nebuchadnezzar's vision of the body with feet of clay:

> England stands but on one foot
> And that has lost one Toe
> Therefore long it cannot stand
> For Foreign troops shall invade our Land.

Jonathan Martin believed that the end was nigh, and the 1830s were the highest point of ruin-neurosis in British history because the mass revival of millennialism coincided with the identification with ancient Rome. Furthermore, in the years leading up to the passage of the Parliamentary Reform Act in 1832 the nation came closer to violent revolution than at any time since the Civil War. After he sold Fonthill Abbey the elderly William Beckford had built a second tower on the hills above Bath, choosing a landscape which reminded him of the Roman Campagna, the 'land of the Dead, strewed with ruins' which he had explored as a Grand Tourist fifty years before. From the tower he could see the fires burning in Bristol, as the crowd rioted in response to the House of Lords' rejection of the Reform Bill. 'I do not wonder at the process of emigration', wrote the disillusioned child of Rousseau and the Enlightenment. 'Flee from the wrath to come is sounding like a blast from the dread trumpet we read of in the Apocalypse. [The Prime Minister] keeps on–on–on– as if advancing to a bed of roses, instead of the gulph of ruins, of despair.'

London was Rome, and Babylon. It had also been Troy. The first Englishman to record a description of the ruins of the city in Asia Minor was Thomas Coryate in *Coryate's Crudities* (1611); he was the countryman from Somerset who walked to India. At Troy he reflected not only on cities such as Nineveh and Babylon but on modern London. 'You may observe . . . one of the most pregnant examples of Luxurie that ever was in the world in these confused heaps of stones. . . . For Adulterie was the principal cause of the ruins of this citie' and London, the new Troy, is 'as much polluted with extravagant lusts as ever was the old Troy'.

Troy is the oldest tourist site in the world, and the scantiness of its remains allowed every traveller to discover the moral he sought. It mattered not a jot that until the middle of the nineteenth century everyone was meditating in the wrong place, mistaking the ruins of the later city of Alexandria Troias for the plains under which Homer's heroes were buried. While Englishmen were fond of the *vanitas* of *Iam seges est ubi Troia fuit*, Julius Caesar and Caracalla had paid homage to the tomb of Achilles; the latter ordered the execution of a favourite so that he could play-act Achilles weeping over the body of his friend Patroclus. In the fourth century the Emperor Julian the Apostate witnessed the veneration of the pagan shrines to Hector and Achilles several decades after Christianity had been proclaimed the state religion; this was evidence, he claimed, that the ancient faith would withstand the Christian cult. The Ottoman Emperor Mehmet the Conqueror made a pilgrimage after capturing Constantinople in 1453 from the Byzantines – descendants of the Greeks – and announced to the ruins, 'I have avenged thee, Asia.'

It was Sultan Mehmet who has given us one of the most remarkable images of ruins as political symbols. He captured Constantinople when he was only twenty-one, and when the flag of the star and the crescent rose above the city on 29 May 1453 it announced the greatest victory in the history of the Ottoman Empire. He entered the city in triumph late in the afternoon, his first priority being to reconsecrate Hagia Sofia as a mosque. Mehmet was awed by the city's architecture, and *en route* he made a diversion to the ruins of the Great Palace on the First Hill. It had been built in the fifth century when Emperor Constantine founded Byzantium, but had been derelict ever since it had been sacked by the Crusaders in the thirteenth century. Mehmet recited a couplet by the Persian poet Saadi:

The spider is the curtain holder in the Palace of the Caesars
The owl hoots its night call on the Towers of Afrasaib.

It was an astonishing moment to pause to consider the fragility of empire. Fires burned in the looted city, women screamed, and the treasures of a thousand years lay waiting on the most triumphant day in the Ottomans' history. Little survives of the Great Palace today. On one side of a narrow wedge of land the railway-lines curve into Istanbul; on the other side is a fortified wall, a six-lane highway and then the sea. Wooden tenements housing Kurdish refugees lead into five vaulted compartments stripped of decoration and at the entrance a junkyard dog barked and snarled, yanking at a rusty chain; I tiptoed past, as that type of chain always snaps in *Just William* stories. It was a bitterly cold day, and the polythene sheets housing homeless beggars under the arches had frozen into stiff wrinkles. I shouted Mehmet's words into the frosty air.

The spider is the curtain holder in the Palace of the Caesars
The owl hoots its night call on the Towers of Afrasaib.

The dog barked, the chain rattled; silence. Saadi's distich was written in the eleventh century AD. In the deserts of the Middle East which were Mehmet's cradle the ruins of older empires cast long shadows. The world's earliest prophecies of future ruin are in the Old Testament. Jeremiah had prophesied Babylon's destruction years before Cyrus invaded in 538 BC, and Zephaniah the fall of Nineveh. When Zephaniah pictured the destruction of the rich and busy metropolis he summoned to mind the images of the ruins of even older civilisations which lay abandoned in the Mesopotamian desert:

> And he [God] will stretch out his hand . . . and destroy
> Assyria; and will make Nineveh a desolation, and dry
> like a wilderness. . . . The cormorant and the bittern
> shall lodge in the upper lintels of it; their voice shall sing
> in the windows; desolation shall be in the thresholds. . . .
> This is the rejoicing city that dwelt carelessly, that said
> in her heart, I am, and there is none beside me: how is
> she become a desolation, a place for beasts to lie down
> in! every one that passeth by her shall hiss, and wag his
> hand.

These biblical prophecies have been enjoyed by many Bible readers travelling to the Middle East. Indeed, the Rev. Henry Maundell would have been thoroughly disappointed to find Tyre plump and thriving when he made a perspiring journey there in 1697:

> A mere Babel of broken walls, pillars, vaults &c., there
> not being so much as one entire house left. Its present
> inhabitants are only a few poor wretches, housing
> themselves in the vaults and subsisting chiefly upon
> fishing; who seem to be preserv'd in this place by Divine
> Providence as a visible argument how God has fulfilled
> his word concerning Tyre, viz, That it should be as the
> top of a rock, a place for fishers to dry their nets on.

While western Europe was the meeting-place of Christian catastrophe and antique exemplar, to understand the politics of the Roman model it is important to appreciate its two faces: as the republic and as the empire. Thomas Jefferson, for example, had admired the early Roman Republic, as did the French Revolutionaries ('Brutus' was the most popular name for baby boys born in France in 1790). But the model was more complex in eighteenth-century England, where Parliament and the Crown replayed the contest for power between Senators and Emperors. The Whigs, who defended the liberties won by Parliament in the previous century, feared that the Crown wished to restore its despotism and that Britons might allow this to happen. Why? Because of the moral corruption of 'Luxury': like the citizens of Rome who had exchanged their liberties for bread and circuses, Britons wanted the luxury goods in the shop windows of the West End. Byron made succinct a hundred years of political theory on the cyclical nature of empires in Canto IV of *Childe Harold*, published in 1818:

> First Freedom, and then Glory – when that fails,
> Wealth – Vice – Corruption, – Barbarism at last.

The earliest warning in poetry was made by John Dyer in *The Ruins of Rome* (1740) when he ascended the hill of the Capitol and imagined the site in the days before its imperial opulence, when its architecture and its politics were each simple, honest and open:

> Britons, O my countrymen beware
> Gird, gird your hearts, the Romans once were free,
> Were brave, were virtuous.

The earliest political commentary in built form was erected by Lord Cobham in his gardens at Stowe in the 1730s. An artificial ruin, his Temple of Modern Virtue faced the intact Temple of Ancient Virtue across a wooded glade. The Temple of Modern Virtue was long ago demolished, Ancient Virtue, erected as a sturdy cylinder of strong masonry, still stands. The juxtaposition of two contrasting temples in the same visual frame was inspired by an article by Joseph Addison in *The Spectator*. He described an allegorical dream of the Elysian Fields. 'The great road lay in a direct line, and was terminated by the temple of Virtue. It was planted on each side with laurels, which were intermixed with marble trophies, carved pillars and statues of law-givers, heroes, statesmen, philosophers and poets.' Next, Addison wrote, he discovered a second Temple whose stones 'were laid together without mortar . . . the whole structure shook with every wind that blew. This was called the temple of Vanity . . . [and] was filled with hypocrites, pedants, free-thinkers, and prating politicians.'

The modern ruin sheltered a headless statue of a man which was rumoured to be the Prime Minister, Sir Robert Walpole. Cobham had been his ally until 1733, when a disagreement over taxation pushed him into opposition. The gardens were open to the public; it was as if *Private Eye* had a garden at the Chelsea Flower Show. The audience was invited to compare the decaying state of morality in modern Britain with the upright virtue of classical antiquity; Walpole's profitable but amoral oligarchy would be the beginning of Britain's decadence, with corruption and moral degeneracy leading inevitably to decadence, decline and invasion by barbarians.

In the course of the century identification with Roman virtue advanced hand in hand with speculation on its vices. After the victorious conclusion of the Seven Years' War in 1763, the generals who had acquired the new empire in America and India were depicted in togas and Roman breastplates, and the Royal Academy of Arts was founded. *London and Westminster Improved* by John Gwynn (1766), one of its founders, was a patriotic blueprint for a neo-classical city as magnificent as Rome, and its rhetoric still echoed in the designs made by Soane, Nash and their pupils fifty years later. To Gwynn, 'The English are now what the Romans were of old, distinguished like them by power and opulence, and excelling all other nations in commerce and navigation. Our wisdom is respected, our laws are envied, and our dominions are spread over a large part of the globe.'

The victorious peace enabled Edward Gibbon to travel to Rome. 'It was at Rome, on the 15th October 1764, as I sat musing amidst the ruins of the Capitol, while the bare-footed friars were singing vespers in the Temple of Jupiter, that the idea of writing the decline and fall of the City first started on my mind.' The Temple of Jupiter was one of the many converted into churches, and it was the juxtaposition of these two civilisations – not the classical monument in pristine isolation – that triggered his intellectual curiosity. In the conclusion to *Decline and Fall* he might have been delineating one of the porticoes erected in the days of Imperial decadence:

> The decline of Rome was the natural and inevitable
> effect of immoderate greatness. Prosperity ripened the
> principles of decay, the causes of destruction multiplied

with the extent of conquest, and as soon as time or
accident had removed the artificial supports, the
stupendous fabric yielded to the pressure of its own
weight.

*Decline and Fall* is a discussion of the past, the present
and the future of Europe. It is not just a book of politics, but
an epic of human nature, argued the literary critic Harold
Bond: 'an 18th-century secular prose equivalent of *Paradise
Lost*'. In Gibbon's view, the citizens of Rome had
squandered their opportunity to realise the full dignity of
man by abandoning their liberties for luxury but the citizens
of eighteenth-century Europe had a second chance to fulfil
this destiny. 'Under the mild and generous influence of
liberty, the Roman empire might have remained invincible
and immortal.' But Rome decayed from within, and would
have fallen with or without the barbarian invasions; like a
rotten tree, it needed only the slightest push.

Only the first third of *Decline and Fall* is the story of
classical Rome. Gibbon's story ends with travellers of
modern times being civilised by their visits to Rome; indeed,
the rediscovery of the ruins might be seen as a form of
redemption. The Europe of our time, wrote Gibbon, is
more prosperous and educated and stable than it has ever
been; like the Comte de Volney in *Les Ruines*, he
represented the Enlightenment optimism that it was
possible to break the cycle of rise, decline and fall. He too
predicted a happy ending. 'Yet the experience of 4,000 years
should enlarge our hopes, and diminish our apprehensions;
we cannot determine to what height the human species may
aspire in their advances towards perfection: but it may safely

be presumed that no people, unless the face of nature is changed, will relapse into their original barbarism.' In the cautiousness of its claims, the reasonableness of its argument, *Decline and Fall* is one of the most optimistic books ever written – and in hindsight, one of the saddest. The final volumes were published in 1788, and by the time Gibbon died in 1794 the demagogic barbarity of the French Revolution had made a bloody mockery of 'liberty'.

The War of American Independence (1775–83) had been the first shock to Britain's growing self-confidence in its empire, however, as expressed in two famous letters by Horace Walpole. 'Our empire is falling to pieces; we are lapsing to a little island', he wrote to one friend in September 1778. Four years earlier he had mused:

> The next Augustan age will dawn on the other side of
> the Atlantic. There will, perhaps, be a Thucydides at
> Boston, a Xenophon at New York, and, in time, a Virgil
> in Mexico, and a Newton at Peru. At last, some curious
> traveller from Lima will visit England and give a
> description of the ruins of St Paul's, like the editions of
> Balbec and Palmyra.

To Lord Charlemont, a young Irishman who visited Athens in 1749, the ruins of Greece exhibited the same lesson of tyranny's triumph over liberty, made all the more vivid when under Turkish rule what had once been the city of Pericles was reduced to a population of a few thousand. Saddest of all was the decline in character of the Greeks: they were indolent and cunning and emasculated in consequence of being ruled by tyrants; unlike the Italians they had produced no Michelangelo, no glimmer of the revival of the ancient spirit. In his journal Charlemont meditated on the despicable hovels:

> Is this the renowned Athens? How melancholy would
> be the reflection should we suppose, what certainly
> must come to pass, that in a few ages hence, London,
> the Carthage, the Memphis, the Athens of the present
> world, shall be reduced to a state like this, and travellers
> shall come, *perhaps from America* [his italics], to view its
> ruins.

Charlemont never published his youthful journal, but we know that at various times he re-edited the manuscript with the benefit of hindsight. In his view, the decline of the British Empire began with the resignation of the elder Pitt in 1761: 'She is fallen!' he wrote in his journal, and when he built the Casino at Marino, a villa outside Dublin, a brass plaque on the foundation stone was dedicated to the administration of William Pitt, 'when the glory of the British Empire arrived at its highest pitch'. It is impossible to prove, but I wonder if Charlemont inserted these prescient remarks on American tourists after the War of Independence.

The best visual illustration of this theme was in a library in Dorset, Merly House, described in a book of engravings published in 1785 by its builder, Ralph Willett, a merchant, book-collector and Fellow of the Society of Antiquaries. Above the door at the entrance to the library was a painting of the Acropolis which visualised Athens in its days of liberty and prosperity, with philosophers discoursing on the steps of the Parthenon and trading vessels unloading in the bay.

*Athens in its State of Ruins,* engraving after a lost painting by Solomon Delane, 1785. Discovering a desolate city ruled by barbarous Turks, English travellers muse on the consequences of exchanging liberty for the seductions of luxury.

Over the exit door was Athens in ruins, with a Muslim minaret commanding the horizon, a woman begging on the crumbling steps of the temple, and the harbour empty of trade. As Turks splinter marble sculptures into fragments for lime, three English travellers – like Charlemont – contemplate the lessons of the scene. Willett added a voice-over: 'Long, very long, may the first picture be the picture of Great Britain; and late, if ever, may the second bear the least resemblance to her sinking state!'

The French Revolution revived the millennialism which

had been dormant during the enlightened century, for the fall of the Bastille was interpreted as one of the signs in the Book of Revelation that announced the Day of Judgement was nigh. In the slums of London the millennialist preacher Richard Brothers thundered that only extreme penance conducted according to his own instructions would dissuade God from destroying this 'spiritual BABYLON'. The Revolution also smashed all political certainties. The monarchical edifice demolished by Napoleon was reassembled by the victors at the Congress of Vienna in 1815 but the brittleness of the repairs was all too visible. In Europe as a whole, according to Professor Schenk in his great book *The Mind of European Romanticism*, apocalyptic fantasies had never been so potent since the late Middle Ages. He quotes a mysterious German writer named F. G. Wetzel who predicted that 'the light will be taken from Europe, [which] will be full of demolished sites, when goblins will meet each other on her desert, and the paradise will have vanished in the great flood and the rage of fire'. An even more mysterious German writer named Schlichtegroll proposed in 1818 to export all of European culture to Iceland where, as if placed in a deep-freeze, it would be preserved from the imminent disaster.

In London the Tory government was trying to resist demands for reform, as we saw earlier, and this political conflict was the catalyst which ignited the fears of millennialists as diverse as Jonathan Martin in Bedlam and William Beckford in Bath. At dinner with the Prime Minister, Lord Liverpool, the French ambassador, Chateaubriand, sent to London by the restored Bourbons, 'praised the solidity of the English monarchy, kept in balance by the even swing of liberty and power'. But Lord Liverpool had doubts: rising and stretching out his arm, the venerable peer 'pointed to the city and said "What sense of solidity can there be with these enormous towns? A serious insurrection in London, and all is lost."' The Prime Minister's foreboding prompted Chateaubriand's reverie that night. 'It seemed to me as though I were finishing a journey to England like that which I made, in earlier days, to the ruins of Athens, of Jerusalem, of Memphis and Carthage.' The England he had explored as an *émigré* exile in the 1790s was 'charming and redoubtable', with 'narrow and gravelled roads, valleys filled with cows, heaths spotted with sheep' overlooked by the steeple of Thomas Gray's country churchyard. Thirty years later

> her valleys are darkened by the smoke of forges and
> workshops. . . . Already the nurseries of knowledge,
> Oxford and Cambridge are assuming a deserted aspect:
> their colleges and Gothic chapels, half-abandoned,
> distress the eye; in their cloisters, near the sepulchral
> stones of the middle ages, lie, forgotten, the marble
> annals of the ancient peoples of Greece: ruins guarding
> ruins.

This widespread despair was the context for 'The New Zealander', a character invented by Thomas Macaulay in a book review (1840) and who quickly acquired a cult following, as represented by Doré's subsequent engraving. But the most astonishing prophecy of destruction is Mary Shelley's novel *The Last Man* (1826). Writing in her widowhood Shelley imagined a mysterious plague from the east which extinguished the population of the known world. The novel is written as prophesying a distant future, Shelley pretending that she has pieced together the words written on the scattered leaves and bark which she and her husband had discovered in an unexplored recess of the cave of the Cumaean Sibyl at Naples; that was in the winter of 1818, shortly before their return to Rome and the writing of *Prometheus Unbound*. Shelley was the model for Adrian, her philosophical King of England, and Byron – also dead by 1826 – for Raymond, his warrior friend. The narrator, Lionel Verney, is in Adrian's retinue as they leave an island extinct of life to search for survivors on the continent. Grass is growing in the silent streets of London, empty of carriages, and 'Birds and tame animals, now homeless, had built nests, and made their lairs in consecrated spots'. Lionel's last glimpse of the great city is of St Paul's dome in the smokeless air; the cathedral has acquired the aspect of a mausoleum, and 'Methought above the portico was engraved the hic jacet of England'.

When Adrian and Lionel reach Venice, Mary Shelley's description is an intensified memory of the winter when she, her husband and Byron had lingered so happily in the deserted, melancholy city. 'The tide ebbed sullenly out from the broken portals and violated halls of Venice: seaweed and sea monsters were left on the blackened marble, while the salt ooze defaced the matchless works of art that adorned their walls, and the sea gull flew out from the shattered window . . . nature asserted her ascendancy.' After a shipwreck, Lionel awakes on the Adriatic shore to find himself 'the Last Man'. Where should the last man alive go but to the world's capital, Time's widow, the 'crown of man's achievements'? In the deserted towns through which he passes he paints on the walls 'Verney, the last of the race of Englishmen, had taken up his abode in Rome'.

The city is silent but for the fountains, and the cows who have returned to the Forum. Wandering through the Vatican, the palaces and the Forum he is consoled by the sight of the greatness of which man is capable, but as night comes he collapses with utter loneliness. He would exchange any masterpiece of art for the chatter of human company. 'I was alone in the Forum; alone in Rome; alone in the world.' Hoping that any fellow survivors would be irresistibly drawn to the Eternal City he climbs the dome of St Peter's to survey the Campagna. But no one appears in the desolation, so at the beginning of the year AD 2100, he deposits the manuscript of 'the Last Man' in the ruins and sails away down the Tiber to search for new life elsewhere.

Verney sails towards the Atlantic. What of the New World during this time of despair? Would it escape what had been described as 'the decrepitude of Europe' by Chateaubriand, who during his own exile had explored its virgin forests? Travelling on a train from London one day I share a table with three Californians who, so I gather, are travelling to the business park at Reading to make a presentation for their hi-tech company. They are tall, broad-shouldered men in their forties, affable, and funny. I write 'America in Ruins' at the top of the page in my notebook. The group's leader glances down and then stares punchily into my eyes, as if considering whether this is an insult. Face to face with the tanned man in the Brooks Brothers shirt at seven o'clock in the morning I certainly feel like the 'decrepitude of Europe'. But there is a serious issue. In the generation after independence in 1784 Americans believed that their nation was God's chosen people and that the New World would be free of decay as if, like an infectious contagion, it could not cross the Atlantic.

Thomas Jefferson studied monuments, not ruins. When he built the Capitol at Richmond, Virginia, he commissioned from Charles-Louis Clérisseau an exact replica of the Temple at Nîmes built by the Romans in the first century AD. What crossed the Atlantic was not a capriccio of mouldering stone, of course, but a plaster model showing the structure in the perfection of its inception. The heroes of the men who signed the Declaration of Independence were the virile, honest Romans of the republic, and not the decadent subjects of the emperors. But what of the next generation? By the 1820s the preachers Lyman Beecher and Andrew Bigelow thundered in the pulpits of New York against 'luxury, the fatal bane of all republics'. It was the beginning of the American School of Catastrophe, and the seeds of a doubt which bloomed in the fallen Statue of Liberty in *Planet of the Apes*, a warning of nuclear apocalypse which was the most astonishing image of ruin in the twentieth century.

Thomas Cole was the first great painter of the American wilderness, an Englishman who was born in Lancashire and emigrated in 1818 at the age of seventeen. Ten years later he was celebrated for his huge canvases of the Catskills and the Hudson River, his depiction of the mighty trees and exhilarating chasms capturing the moment at which man caught his breath at the wonder of Nature. Nature was God's creation, and Americans the people chosen to cultivate its magnificence.

Cole made a journey to Italy in 1832. 'The traveller is unworthy of his privilege, and forgetful of his duty, if he extracts not from the scenes some moral lesson or religious truth', he wrote, stating what was taken for granted by contemporaries but has been forgotten today. His first moral lesson in Rome was the 'effeminacy of modern Europe' which was symbolised by the labourers who were shovelling earth from the ruins, for excavations in the Forum had now begun. The dilatoriness of the scrawny, idle labourers who shovelled away the earth was all the more remarkable when one considered that their heroic ancestors had raised the massive structures which now appeared in all their might. Cole told his parents: 'You would laugh to see modern Roman labourers *at work*', in contrast to the labourers back home. 'Their wheel-barrows were as large as a shovel-full and were pushed ten yards before they rest, and if a clod is earth as big as a fist they break it before attempting to lift.'

To a strong, young American they represented the decrepitude of Europe. More profoundly, it was there that – like Gibbon, and like Volney at Palmyra – he had an epiphanic vision of the cyclical nature of empires. A party of Americans surveyed the Forum at sunset. Cole 'unusual for him, was the first to speak, recalled a friend who was present. 'The subject was that of the future course of Empire . . . until he closed with a picture that found its parallel in the melancholy desolation by which, at that moment, they were surrounded. Such was Cole, the poet artist, in Rome . . .' On his return to New York he was commissioned by a rich man named Luman Reed to paint five great canvases on the theme for his New York apartment. *The Course of Empire*

began with a wooded seashore at dawn inhabited only by
wild beasts; the second scene depicted an Arcadian idyll of
hunters, shepherds and farmers felling trees to plant corn
and erect the first huts. At noonday we see the empire in
its dazzling glory, a city of bronze statues and marble
colonnades with trading vessels in the blue bay and a
military triumph crossing the scene. Then came destruction,
in Cole's words 'towers falling, arches broken, vessels
wrecking in the harbour'. The canvas was painted in the
manner of John Martin's *Fall of Babylon*, and the decadent
populace flee a catastrophic storm, flames and a vengeful
invading army. The story ends at sunset with 'a desolate
ruin', the ruined colonnades reclaimed by Nature as the
scene reverts to a wild seashore. There are no human figures,
and the only voice is that of a solitary bird. 'This picture
must be as the funeral knell of departed greatness,' Cole told
his client, 'and may be called the state of desolation.'

The scene echoed that sunset in Rome. In Cole's view of
history, the United States stood at the transition from the
taming of the wilderness in the mid-morning to the imperial
dazzle at noon; it was brunch, one might say, and time for
New Yorkers to change their ways. Cole, a Methodist, was
already disillusioned by the dark underside of the American
dream, disturbed at seeing not only the growing 'luxury'
of the cities but also the economic exploitation of the
wilderness by lumber mills and factories. Later in the 1830s
a railway was built in the valley below his summer house in
the Catskills, despoiling a valley whose virgin beauty Cole
had made famous; in a canvas now in the Metropolitan
Museum, he painted the view once more but ignored the
railway. The luminosity of the river and its meadows is all

the more radiant, for Cole had abandoned his hope in Americans as God's chosen people and retreated into a golden, imaginary past. When he had sailed to Europe in 1832 he held in his pocket an ode dedicated to him by Asher Durand, who had eulogised in poetry the wilderness which Cole had celebrated in paint. The ode begged his friend Cole not to be contaminated by the European disease of ruin, but Cole was not the first or last tourist from the New World to succumb to the contagious malaise of the Old.

The first American citizen to study the ruins of Greece was a nineteen-year-old scholar from Philadelphia, Nicholas Biddle. He was born in 1785, the year after Independence, and as a scion of one of the leading families in New England was as carefully moulded to fulfill his nation's destiny as a tennis player might be today. He arrived in Europe with no doubts as to the superiority of America; the 'coming people' of his native state were the best in the world, he declared. It was the monuments of Athens which decided Biddle to become a statesman, because they demonstrated what could be achieved by argument and debate in a society of men who were educated and free. Eloquence had built these temples of marble, he believed. I imagine Biddle as a slim, young figure in a linen suit contemplating the Parthenon; if we turn from the dazzling marble to face him we see in his eyes the forests, homesteads and towns of the New World.

Taken by themselves a nineteen-year-old's views on an archaeological site are of no value; their interest is in their application to the future America. Biddle was not interested in modern Europe, whose cities were oppressed by the 'pompous glare' of tyrants' palaces. 'The present generation of men is more civilised, more enlightened, better than any

of these whose exploits are transmitted by history . . . if I am
not biased by affection, the coming people of Pennsylvania
will be as good as any in [Europe].' Reaching Italy he
considered the modern Romans degenerate, striving 'to
hide behind a luxurious profusion the loss of the primitive
virtues of their country'. The Athenians were even more
wretched, but somehow the very extinction of the city made
it more inspiring to an American:

> Whilst therefore we feel at Rome a mingled sentiment
> of melancholy and admiration, Athens reflects the
> perfect picture of desolation and despair . . . Rome is
> the twilight, Athens the black night of ruin. . . . The
> religion of Athens is lost forever. Her temples which
> have resisted not only the barbarous rage of conquest,
> but the frenzy of the elements, now moulder under the
> hand of ignorance or idle curiosity, and on the noblest
> structures of Paganism a Turkish mosque has raised its
> solitary spire (shapeless column) to mock the elegance
> of Grecian arts and to proclaim the victory of a new
> religion.

Thus he wrote to his brother in June 1806, referring to
the mosque and minaret built inside the Parthenon.

> Her crowded theatres are deserted. . . . Where are her
> people? Are these few wretches, scarcely superior to the
> beasts whom they drive heedlessly over the ruins, are
> these men Athenians? Where is her freedom? Ah! This is
> the keenest stab of all. Bowed down by a foul
> oppression, the spirit of Athens has bent under its

slavery. . . . One solitary sail in the Piraeus tells the sad
story of Athenian misery. It is thus by collecting the
scattered images of greatness and decay, we become
interested in the misfortunes of a nation, and we are
instructed in the melancholy but pleasing philosophy of
ruins.

In Biddle's journal there is a sense – a confused sense,
admittedly – of having discovered the fragmentary but
pristine pieces of marble which will serve as building blocks
for the foundations of a new society. As he wrote, however,
Lord Elgin's agents had begun to remove the marble
sculptures from the pediment for shipment to London.
Biddle was furious, but not because the British were robbing
Greece: they were robbing America. Biddle claimed ancient
Athens as the inspiration for his generation, and he wished
them to remain *in situ* for future Americans to study the
same moral lesson.

Sadly, Biddle never realised his ideals. He became
president of the US Bank, but never the President of his
country, and his enlightened view of federalism was
destroyed by the demagoguery of Andrew Jackson. He is
best remembered for introducing the Greek Revival style of
architecture to banks in America, and on the streets of
Philadelphia was called 'Nick the Greek', a nickname which
to modern ideas has a slightly gangsterish ring. Biddle had
been deceived by the ruins of Greece, in two senses. First,
eloquence was not enough in politics. Second, and more
subtly, he had interpreted the survival of Athens's
monuments as a demonstration of the ultimate triumph of
democracy. Visiting Sparta he was uplifted by the sight of a

completely empty plain, for the disappearance of the
monuments of a military tyranny gave 'a republican a
melancholy pleasure. My own country offers an interesting
analogy of which I have thought much.'

An analogy he did not predict was that made in Taylor
Lewis's *State Rights: A Photograph from the Ruins of Ancient
Greece* published in 1865, the year the American Civil War
ended. Photographing the charred skeletons of the cities
burned on Sherman's march through Georgia, the
northerner Lewis used history to argue the triumph of his
cause. 'God has given us a mirror in the past . . . all the dire
calamities of Greece' can be explained by the individual
states' desire for autonomy. But not only had Biddle failed
to predict his own nation's destiny, he had misread the
language of ruins itself. Writing at the end of the fifth
century BC the historian Thucydides had predicted Biddle's
visit. The Spartans 'occupy two-fifths of the Peloponnese',
he said, but if the city 'became deserted and only the temples
and foundations of buildings remained, I think that future
generations would, as time passed, find it very difficult to
believe that the place had really been as powerful . . .
[because] the city is not regularly planned and contains no
temples or monuments of great magnificence'. Sparta had
disappeared because its soldier rulers had little interest in
architectural lavishness. If, on the other hand, 'the same
thing were to happen to Athens, one would conjecture from
what met the eye that the city had been twice as powerful as
in fact it is'. Athens would survive, Thucydides argued, not
because it was greater than Sparta but because its rulers were
more interested in architecture.

Monuments are deceptive, and in posterity doubly so. In

The antique statue 'Pasquino', near the church of S Pantaleo.

an alley near Piazza Navona stands the mutilated head and torso of an antique statue, nicknamed Pasquino. Pasquino shows that ruins do not speak; we speak for them. From the sixteenth century onwards Roman citizens pinned written satires to the base of the statue, and a 'pasquinade' became the name for an attack on the Establishment. In time the plinth was inscribed:

> But I am that famous Pasquino
> Who makes the great lords tremble
> And astonishes foreigners and countrymen
> When I compose in vernacular or Latin.

No one would pin satires to Pasquino were he as lofty, proud and assertive as the Apollo Belvedere, or a Horse-Tamer on the Quirinal. But as he is fallen and battered we put our words into his mouth.

The same ship which brought the ruins of Leptis Magna to Britain also carried the colossal granite head of an Egyptian prince, which had been hauled across the desert from the temple at Thebes. It was the head of Ramases II we now know, but when it was unveiled at the British Museum in March 1818 some called him 'Ozymandias'. The sight of the head of the fallen tyrant inspired the finest sonnet Shelley ever wrote:

> I met a traveller from an antique land
> Who said: Two vast and trunkless legs of stone
> Stand in the desert. . . . Near them, on the sand,
> Half sunk, a shattered visage lies, whose frown,
> And wrinkled lip, and sneer of cold command,
> Tell that its sculptor well those passions read
> Which yet survive, stamped on these life less things,
> The hand that mocked them, and the heart that fed:
> And on the pedestal these words appear:
> 'My name is Ozymandias, king of kings:
> Look on my works, ye Mighty, and despair!'
> Nothing beside remains. Round the decay
> Of that colossal wreck, boundless and bare
> The lone and level sands stretch far away.

# X

# Dust in the Air Suspended

Inside the Alcázar of Toledo, once a palace of the kings of Spain, is a small room which is as frozen in time as Miss Havisham's house. The study of Colonel Moscardo is preserved at the moment tragedy struck, on 23 July 1936. Wallpaper hangs in shreds from the ceiling, and the walls are riddled with bullet-holes dribbling plaster. In the centre is the colonel's desk, and on the desk a black telephone filmy with dust. When the visitor pushes a button the telephone rings three times.

LUIS MOSCARDO    Papa!
COLONEL MOSCARDO   What's happening, son?
LUIS They say they're going to shoot me if you don't surrender.
MOSCARDO    Then commend your soul to God, shout *Viva España!* and *Viva Cristo El Rey!* And die like a hero.

Luis was sixteen years old, and the Colonel's only son. 'Adiós, Papa, un bacio muy fuerte' – 'a big kiss', he said – and seconds later was shot by the Republican militia.

The four-square mass of the Alcázar crowns the hill on which Toledo is built, and shares with the Gothic spire of the cathedral a skyline made famous by El Greco. By the end of the Civil War siege the cathedral was still intact but there was no Alcázar: it had been battered to the ground. The Renaissance fortress was serving as a barracks for trainee cadets when in the summer of 1936 the Nationalists rebelled against the elected Socialist government. Toledo was loyal, and Colonel Moscardo found himself inside the fortress with twelve hundred teenage soldiers surrounded by several thousand militia, who were shooting nuns and priests in the streets. On the third day of the siege the militia found Luis. It was then that their commander telephoned the Alcázar.

The colonel's sacrifice of his only son gave the cadets the resolve to survive shelling and starvation, retreating deeper into the cellars as each day another Renaissance arcade fell to shell-fire. The battle in Spain's archbishopric became so significant a symbol to Franco's 'crusade' that he diverted his armies from the advance on Madrid. Toledo was recaptured after sixty days of the siege, and his troops shot or stabbed any man suspected of bearing a rifle for the militia. The steps of the steep, narrow streets ran with waterfalls of blood. It is hard to imagine the brutality of civil war in the tranquil city today. The square in which Luis was executed has stalls selling the nuttiest marzipan in Spain, and the streets are crowded with tourists on the El Greco pilgrimage.

After the war the Alcázar was rebuilt as an exact facsimile. Franco's obsession was the appearance of unity, and this reconstruction symbolised that of Spain. In the courtyard the bronze statue of the Emperor Charles V crushing heresy in the form of a serpent was put back on the plinth from which it had been toppled. Spain stood four-square to the

world again, having withstood the disloyalty of a minority of
Communists. The cracks were invisible: as invisible as the
tens of thousands of Republicans in prison camps, or toiling
underground to construct the vast chamber inside the
mountains west of Madrid which commemorated the
Nationalist martyrs of the conflict.

Moscardo's sacrifice of his only son was central to this
myth. His study had been on the one side of the courtyard
which survived, and it was preserved as a bullet-riddled
shrine. The only insertions are full-length portraits of the
father and son, and a frieze of marble plaques on which the
conversation is transcribed in twenty languages. English
fathers and sons do not kiss each other, however, so in this
translation the boy held at gunpoint sounds a little as if it is
the first day of term at prep school: 'All my fondest love,
Father.' 'All of mine to you.'

Tourists unaware of the politics see only a father and son,
and leave the room with moist eyes. For Spaniards the room
is a problem, however, a time-capsule of their Civil War. It
is impossible to gauge as to where the sympathies of the
elderly visitors lie but those brought up after Franco's death
in 1975 avoid the room: it is *macabro*, 'creepy'. The return
of democracy to Spain was based upon a *pacto de olvido*, 'a
pact of forgetting', which meant drawing a curtain over the
past by mutual agreement. Francoist monuments were not
toppled, and Moscardo's study was left in peace. It would be
too controversial to restore such a room, however, so the
ruin is lightly cleaned once a week but never repaired.
Wallpaper peels, and plaster crumbles. The fossilised
memories of Moscardo's sacrifice will disappear into the
cleaning lady's vacuum cleaner.

Colonel Moscardo's study raises the two problems of the ruins of wartime. First, how to preserve in perpetuity a moment of destruction: the tragic purity of the flames, the hushed silence and rubble of a bomb site, and the cloud of the fine debris that hung in the air before gently settling on your clothes. 'Dust in the air suspended / Marks the place where the story ended', wrote T. S. Eliot in *Little Gidding*, having served as an air-raid warden in the Second World War.

Second, who decides the moral of the story? The seductiveness of the shrine in Toledo led an English socialist named Herbert Rutledge Southworth to investigate further, and in 1964 he published *The Myth of the Crusade of Franco*. Moscardo had another son killed in the war, Southworth argued, but not in these circumstances. Luis Moscardo, he claimed, was alive and well and living in Madrid. His address was No. 48 Calle de Castellón. Monuments of military victory are particularly deceptive. In Cuba, for example, the prelude to Fidel Castro's uprising was an assault in 1953 on the Moncada Barracks in Santiago. It was a fiasco, and he and his guerrillas were imprisoned for the next five years. The military government filled the bullet-holes in the façade with cement, to erase the memory. After Castro returned to seize power, however, the wall was machine-gunned a second time and preserved as one of the holy shrines of the revolution.

After the two world wars in Europe there was a much bigger problem. First and foremost, what was to be done with the rubble caused by high-explosive bombs and shells? It is a society's aspirations for peacetime that determine whether a ruin is rebuilt, replaced, or preserved – or, rather,

the rulers' interpretations of society's wishes. After the First
World War Winston Churchill proposed that the town of
Ypres should be preserved as a blackened skeleton, an open-
air monument to the British dead. It was rebuilt, however,
and the facsimile of the great medieval Cloth Hall was an
assertion of the triumph of an older culture over a recent
barbarism. Einstein toured the battlefields of northern
France in order to publicise the cause of peace, and was
photographed in the ruins declaring that all the young men
in the world should visit the rubble to be cured for ever of
the romantic approach to war inspired by literature: 'If only
they could see what I see,' he declared.

After the Second World War, of course, the problem was
increased by the same factor as was the power of high
explosive. Hiroshima was rebuilt, but the monument to the
nuclear explosion was designed to appear as if its domed
ceiling was suspended at the point of collapse. In Poland
historic palaces and churches were rebuilt as defiant, perfect
replicas because the dynamiting of the nation's architectural
heritage had been one of the Nazis' weapons in a systematic
programme to obliterate Polish culture. The Russians, by
contrast, were the only Allied victors to glorify the ruins of
their enemies. The official artist Deinecka painted a bomber
of inviolable glassiness flying over the blackened shell of
the Reichstag in 1945, from the windows of which fluttered
a red flag. In Berlin, the new Communist government
demolished the Schluler Schloss, a residence of the Prussian
monarchy and thus a symbol of imperialist aggression. They
preserved, however, a slender vertical section of wall that
supported the balcony from which Rosa Luxemburg had
proclaimed the short-lived Socialist Republic of Germany in

1917. There are a hundred more examples in Europe alone but although each human tragedy is unique, the architectural expression is a variation upon a familiar dialogue of fragmentation versus wholeness.

Perhaps the most instructive example is the Frauenkirche, or Church of Our Lady, in Dresden. Goethe climbed inside the dome of this Baroque masterpiece to view a city which claimed to be the most beautiful in Germany. On the nights of 13 and 14 February 1945 Dresden was bombed by Allied aeroplanes and its citizens died in the storm of fire. The city was as burned out as a photographic negative. It was rebuilt, with the exception of the Frauenkirche. When the western Allies became the enemies of Soviet Russia, the Communist authorities decided to preserve its ruins as a reminder of 'capitalist warmongering'. The dome which had been so admired by Goethe, so glorious and uplifting in its height and glittering transparency, was left as a slag-heap of blackened stones. But the people of Dresden placed lit candles in the rubble as a spontaneous protest year after year: they did not want their children's growth – or their own old age – to be stunted by the dark shadow of history. As soon as the Berlin Wall came down they began to rebuild the Frauenkirche to its original design and once again it stands in beautiful, intact solemnity; a spontaneous resurrection. The original stones were reused wherever possible, and as Britain's millennium gift to Germany a London blacksmith whose father had flown a bomber in the raids was commissioned to make the golden ball and cross which crown the dome. And inside Russia itself the German government is now rebuilding several of the churches they destroyed in the invasion of 1941 as a form of diplomatic penance.

At the opposite end of the spectrum are the ruins of Oradour-sur-Glane, a deserted village near Limoges in the south-west of France. In the hedgerows at the entrance to the village – where in England you would read PLEASE DRIVE CAREFULLY – signs have been placed instructing SILENCE and REMEMBER.

On 10 June 1944 Oradour had a population of 650 men, women and children. Between four and five-thirty p.m., soldiers of an SS Panzer division machine-gunned the men in rows and locked the women and children inside the church, where they were burned alive. Today a bird's nest perches on the parapet of its ruined shell and placed on the altar is the twisted metal skeleton of a child's pram. In the crypt below are displayed the relics of ordinary lives: charred banknotes, saucepans whose handles have drooped with the heat, wrist-watches with their hands stopped at the moment when their wearers were shot. Outside in the market-place is the oxidised husk of the saloon car driven by the local doctor and a postcard is available labelled '*Voiture du Docteur Dessourteaux*'.

In an article about these ruins, published on 28 November 1998, the journalist Michael McMahon admits to an uncomfortable sense of intruding upon a tragedy that is incomprehensible to us. More disturbingly, friends who visited recently described how a man was walking through the church in football shorts with his eye pressed to the viewfinder of a video camera. Oradour has become a tourist attraction, and it will never again be as silent as the morning after 10 June. No artistic intervention could create such images as the doctor's rusted car or the melted pram, but would Oradour have been more poignant if it was allowed to slowly crumble into oblivion? Perhaps in this case a stark, frozen, lifeless memorial is indeed more useful than a ruin with a deceptively gentle promise of transition.

Britain is the one country in Europe whose response was not a variation upon the theme above. At the height of the Blitz Kenneth Clark declared that 'Bomb damage is in itself Picturesque'. This could only have been said in Britain. As chairman of the War Artists Advisory Committee (WAAC) – and director of the National Gallery, and also the guiding intellect of contemporary art – Clark commissioned artists such as John Piper and Graham Sutherland to paint the glowing embers of the bomb sites in which more than 13,000 people died in the five months from September 1940 alone.

Clark's first book had been *The Gothic Revival*, in which he had dubbed follies in landscape gardens as 'monuments to a mood'. Together with cultural luminaries, including T. S. Eliot and John Maynard Keynes, he signed a letter to *The Times* on 15 August 1944 proposing that a number of bombed churches should be preserved in ruins as war memorials. They would be monuments to the mood of the Blitz, and would stand to remind a new generation of 'the sacrifice on which [their] apparent security has been built'. The project was elaborated in a book with drawings by Barbara Jones and detailed designs by architects such as Hugh Casson. *Bombed Churches as War Memorials* is the last great fling of the British Picturesque, summoning the spirit of Stourhead and Stowe to soothe the trauma of high-explosive bombs. These churches would not be cold, black slag-heaps of unforgiving bitterness, as at Dresden, but garden ruins haunted by birds and soft with greenery, places that children would be thrilled to explore. Stone colonnades truncated by the blast would continue as rows of trees, and roofless crypts become sunken, sheltered gardens.

The authors accepted that the great majority of churches would be rebuilt or demolished, but they suggested six

*Bombed Churches as War Memorials*: St Alban's, Wood Street. In 1945 artists proposed to preserve a number of bombed churches in the city as memorials to the Blitz – and as places to assemble for open-air service.

whose ruins would be of particular potency. In the first place, they would continue as sanctuaries for midday prayer in the open air. In a drawing of St Alban's, Wood Street, we see Londoners in light jackets listen to a preacher who stands on a plinth, dressed in a surplice. Secondly, these garden ruins would be open spaces, 'glimpses of green against the livid grey of pavement and buildings'. Thirdly, they would be memorials:

> It will not be many years before all traces of war damage will have gone, & its strange beauty vanished from our streets. No longer will the evening sky be reflected in the water-pools which today lie dark and quiet between torn and gaping walls. Soon a pockmarked parapet or a broken cornice will be to future generations the only sign of former shock and flame. The shabby heap of stones, flowering with willow-herbs as pink and lively as the flames which earlier sprouted from their crevices, will disappear, and with their going the ordeal which we passed will seem remote, unreal, perhaps forgotten. Save us, then, some of our ruins.

The proposal is 'Picturesque' because it recognises that the creation of a meditative atmosphere requires an artist's eye:

> Preservation is not wholly the archaeologist's job: it involves an understanding of the ruin as a ruin, and its re-creation as a work of art in its own right. . . . A ruin is more than a collection of debris. It is a place with its own individuality, charged with its own emotion and atmosphere and drama, of grandeur, of nobility, or of

charm. These qualities must be preserved as carefully as
the broken stones which are their physical embodiment.

The designs were not followed, however, and the ruins
which were preserved seem to be tidy, accidental leftovers
with all those features of the corporation aesthetic – mown
grass, KEEP OFF signs and trim shrubberies – which the
writers had specifically opposed. Christ Church in Newgate
Street in the City was preserved as two walls of a nave open
to a dual carriageway. Gravel paths delineate the missing
walls, rose bushes record the columns of the nave. In 1958,
John Betjeman, who remembered worshipping in the
church, paused at the scene in his 'Monody on the Death of
Aldersgate Street Station':

Last of the east sculpture, a cherub gazes
On broken arches, rosebays, bracken and dock
Where once I heard the roll of the Prayer Book phrases
And the sumptuous tick of the old west gallery clock.

On sunny days Christ Church is now a pleasant green oasis,
and when there is a pause in the noise of the traffic there are
few places in London which are closer to the reverential
silence of 1945: many have found lessons here of survival
and regeneration. But in the cold and rain, contemplation is
harder – and perhaps the ruins should be left a little wilder.
A recent television programme filmed two street cleaners
working in the City of London. 'What the Corporation
hates', said one, spraying weed-killer into cracks in an old
wall, 'is *grass*.'

'No longer will the evening sky be reflected in the water-pools which today lie dark and quiet between torn and gaping walls. Soon a pockmarked parapet or a broken cornice will be to future generations the only sign of former shock and flame': the 'strange beauty' which the authors of *Bombed Churches as War Memorials* wished to preserve was better captured in the paintings of John Piper. He painted Christ Church hours after its bombing in December 1940. It is a painting liquid with heat, the sacredness of the church somehow intensified in its destruction. To the lover of ruins Piper's paintings are the greatest works inspired by the events of the war. He did not choose to depict bomb sites, but was dispatched to them by order of the Ministry of Information, through the WAAC, which commissioned more than 4,000 pictures during the course of the war, the majority depicting dog-fights, brave firemen, and sailors on the shimmering decks of battleships. The pictures were to be a record, and a boost to morale. Clark admitted later that a third, undisclosed aim of the programme was to prevent artists being killed.

Piper's first painting of a bomb site was made in Coventry. The city was flattened by four hundred German bombers on 15 November 1940 and the next day fires were still burning and bodies being stretchered from the rubble. Piper was at a loss what to do, embarrassed at the sense of intruding upon such tragedy with a sketching pad. Then he noticed a brass plate on a door which stood intact beside the cathedral. He recognised this as a solicitor's office; his father had been a solicitor. 'It was a port in a storm', he was later to recall. At a window inside a secretary was typing away 'as if nothing had happened'. 'I said "Good morning. It's a beastly time, isn't it?" And she explained that she had only

*Coventry Cathedral, 15 November 1940* by John Piper. Piper was one of the artists commissioned by the British government to depict bomb damage. The morning after the Germans raided Coventry he painted the ruins of St Michael's in an image which became 'Britain's Guernica'.

just come on duty. I told her I had been ordered to do some drawings. She said "Of course, you can have my place". She moved her typewriter to the other side of the room and I started drawing the Cathedral.'

Her window faced the east end of the Gothic structure. In the painting we seem to see the apse through a shimmering haze of heat, the stone tracery – which remained intact in reality – dissolving like wood-ash. The cathedral still burns in this canvas, and through the tracery we see white light, as if the high altar is radiating spirituality. Piper did not invent the colours in his paintings, explains David Fraser Jenkins, the only writer to illuminate their relationship to the author's enigmatic personality. Studying a scene he chose from its spectrum of colours those which seemed to represent its inner spirit, and intensified them. The pictures are as empty of figures as designs for stage-sets, but he succeeded in projecting a human agony in that intensity of colour, and in the scratching of the knife on the canvas. Their conviction can only be explained by the pain he felt.

The Coventry picture was exhibited at the National Gallery in an exhibition of WAAC work later that year and this small painting, Jenkins explains, became for Britons what Picasso's *Guernica* had been for loyalist Spaniards: an expression of British resilience. Piper was suddenly popular with the general public, although his style was highly avant-garde. Bath, his favourite city, was bombed in April 1942 precisely because of its architectural beauty: in retaliation for Britain's destruction of the medieval quarter of Bremen, the Luftwaffe chose new targets from their Baedeker guides. 'I went to Bath to paint bomb damage', Piper wrote to John Betjeman, his close friend, on 15 May 1942:

> I never was sent to do anything so sad before. I was
> miserable there indeed to see that haunt of ancient

water-drinkers besmirched with dust and blast. 3 houses
burnt out in Royal Crescent, bomb in middle of Circus,
and 2 burnt out there; Lansdown Chapel direct hit, 10
bombs in front of Lansdown Crescent, Somerset Place
almost completely burnt out; a shell . . . 326 killed,
1800 houses made uninhabitable. . . . My God I did
hate that week.

It is because of this anguish that these water-colours were
Piper's finest works of the war, argued Betjeman.

When he was not working for the Ministry of Information, Piper chose older ruins to paint. Seaton Delaval
was a country house near Newcastle which had been built in
1718 to the designs of Sir John Vanbrugh and lain derelict
since a fire in 1822. As the artist described in an article he
wrote for *Orion* magazine in 1945 the house was
surrounded by colliery tips, and miners with lamps on their
hats walked home down the long avenue. A farmer grew hay
in the forecourt, and troops were quartered in its 'boarded-
up, floorless saloons':

Ochre and flame-licked red, pock-marked and stained in
purplish umber and black, the colour is extremely up-
to-date: very much of our times. And not the colour
only. House and landscape are seared by the east wind,
and riven with fretting industrialism, but they still
withstand the noise and neglect, the fires and hauntings
of twentieth-century life. Its main block an untenanted
stone shell, the Hall is somehow alive, unlike many
stately homes.

*Seaton Delaval* by John Piper, 1941. Left to his own devices, Piper chose older ruins – such as the gutted shell of this mansion in Northumberland – to symbolise the resilience of the British character.

Seaton Delaval should remain a stubborn, unpolished ruin, and be enjoyed by rowdy Bank Holiday crowds rather than National Trust members, he concluded. He painted how the fire of 1822 'leapt in tongues of flame affectionately round Vanbrugh's mouldings, staining the stone permanently red and purple'. The canvas, in the Tate, is as knobbly in relief as a surface of cork, so globby is the oil paint – black for the charred mouldings, a shapeless red flickering across the surface – and so deep the gouges made by the palette knife. This was a 'magnificent modern ruin', which seemed to prophesy the new beauty of post-war Britain.

In an article of 1948 entitled 'Pleasing Decay' he wrote of 'the recent ascendancy of the archaeologist's influence, and the diminishing figure of the artist [in ruins] . . . the artist and the archaeologist with an eye must regain influence or all will be lost'. He continued by saying that Picasso and Max Ernst 'prophesied the beauty as well as the horror of bomb damage, and as visual planners they are at the moment unrivalled. Bomb damage has revealed new beauties in unexpected appositions.' The words conjure up an architecture of transparency, of fractured colliding perspectives, but it was not until the 1990s that architects such as Frank Gehry and Daniel Libeskind showed that architecture could achieve such excitement of form. In Coventry the architects of the 1950s built a new cathedral adjacent to the old, and the ruined apse painted by Piper was preserved as a fire-blackened memento. Round it is a new city centre. But the architects failed to translate the vivacity of paint into concrete and glass; Piper's painting – even if just a postcard reproduction in your pocket – is more alive and warm than the cold, grey, inhabited blocks of concrete.

Is it ever possible to preserve the 'strange beauty' of war, to capture the moment of 'dust in the air suspended'? Yes, as demonstrated by the ruins of Orford Ness on the Suffolk coast. Until the 1970s this was a secret weapons testing centre of the Ministry of Defence (MoD). The site faces the village of Orford, with the rock-like keep of the castle built by Henry II in 1152. The Ness is not an island, in fact, but the head of a long neck of shingle which for 12 miles runs parallel to the marshy coast south of Aldeburgh, preventing the River Ade from turning out to sea like a left-back jostling a winger down the touchline. This spit is a geological phenomenon, formed by the wind and tide in the course of thousands of years.

In the First World War the RAF tested the accuracy of aerial bombing on the deserted beaches of the Ness, its shingle ideal for deadening the impact of the explosions. In the 1930s some of the earliest experiments into radar were conducted here, and during the Second World War British firepower was tested on the fuselages of captured enemy aircraft. In the 1950s the MoD began to test explosive triggers for nuclear bombs and constructed massive chambers on the seashore, upturned concrete hulls whose flanks were heaped with hundreds of tons of shingle as extra protection. The Ness became one of the most secret places in Britain, inaccessible to villagers, the jaunty young boffins in shirt-sleeves who had played at radar in the open air replaced by the sinister, silent bunkers on the grey horizon. Labs 4 and 5 were dubbed the 'Pagodas' because of their silhouette, as if they were follies in a garden. Each Pagoda's roof is raised on slender piers, like a rowing eight carrying their boat above their heads. No one knew the purpose of the design: that if there was an accidental detonation, the legs would fall away and the roof would slam down as a colossal lid capping the blast.

In the 1970s the MoD departed, leaving the Ness to the local fishermen and the few walkers who were not unsettled by the bunkers' menacing lethality. The site was acquired by the National Trust in 1993 for its value to Britain's coastline and the immediate thought was to demolish the bunkers. It was Jeremy Musson, an architectural historian working for the Trust at that time, who first argued their value as ruins. The Ness of shifting shingle, he said, was a palimpsest of twentieth-century history, from the wooden huts of the First World War to the Cold War's Pagodas. In a new and hopefully more peaceful century the ruins would crumble into extinction in exposure to the wind and waves, as if the earth was being purified by Nature.

The National Trust adopted this approach, a brave decision when one considers the regulations on health and safety, and the expectations of members accustomed to tea-rooms, and upholstery, and precisely placed furniture. I hope they remain as brave, because there is only a handful of examples in Europe – Orford Ness is one, Ninfa another – of sites which demonstrate that if a ruin's owner is guided by an artistic vision then it can be opened to the public with its strange magic undiluted. Here too the approach was that of the eighteenth-century Picturesque: that is to say, a per-spective which 'framed' the experience of visiting but also involved a moral narrative, and a meditation on time, transience and humanity. As in an eighteenth-century landscape garden, a painter was involved at the conceptual stage. Dennis Creffield, an admirer of Turner – who had painted the medieval castle – camped in a wooden hut and rose at dawn to depict an island in which distance and scale were impossible to estimate, the air unnaturally thin and luminous, and on days of sunshine the shingle shimmering and rippling as if the Ness were a transient mirage. Musson notes that Creffield's pictures influenced the Trust in its presentation of the site, the management team soon recognising that the painter understood better than anyone the 'mood, moment and the unexpected music of the island which hangs between the calling gulls and the endless wind'.

Visit today, and you take a boat across the muddy,

Orford Ness, photograph by W. G. Sebald, in *The Rings of Saturn*.
Inside the 'pagodas' on the shingle at Orford Ness, Suffolk,
scientists of the Cold War tested the triggers of nuclear bombs.

sluggish River Ade at high tide. Few plants can take root
here, and the life of Nature is represented by the wind
whipping the grey sea on to the shore, flinging the shingle
at the concrete walls, and oxidising the rusty coils of wire,
jagged metal and snapped railway-lines. Or by the rabbits
and hares, and the flocks of gulls with windy cries which nest
on the laboratories. Half-buried by shingle, the labs seem
half-man, half-Nature. The interiors of these shells are as
banal as any industrial desolation, with scaffolds, ramps,
channels of slimy, green water, and the rusty metal plates on
which charges were detonated. The Cold War is over.

Orford Ness still lives up to the description of a great
writer who discovered the site in its neglected loneliness.
*The Rings of Saturn* by W. G. Sebald (1995) describes the
author's walk along the coasts of Norfolk and Suffolk,
meditating on the transience of man's imposition on the
landscape and observing the inhabitants with the bemused

clarity of an alien. Sebald described his reverie in haunting, pebble-smooth prose. The walker pays a villager to ferry him across to an island 'which resembled a penal colony in the Far East':

> From a distance, the concrete shells, shored up with stones, in which for most of my lifetime hundreds of boffins had been at work devising new weapons systems, looked (probably because of their odd conical shape) like the tumuli in which the mighty and powerful were buried in prehistoric times with all their tools and utensils, silver and gold. My sense of being on ground intended for purposes transcending the profane was heightened by a number of buildings that resembled temples or pagodas, which seemed quite out of place in these military installations. But the closer I came to these ruins, the more any notion of a mysterious isle of the dead receded, and the more I imagined myself amidst the remains of our own civilisation after its extinction in some future catastrophe. To me too, as for some latter-day stranger ignorant of the nature of our society wandering about among heaps of scrap metal and defunct machinery, the beings who had once lived and worked here were an enigma, as was the purpose of the primitive contraptions and fittings inside the bunkers, the iron rails under the ceilings, the hooks on the still partially tiled walls, the showerheads the size of plates, the ramps and soakaways. Where and in what time I truly was that day at Orfordness I cannot say, even now as I write these words. All I do know is that I finally walked along the raised embankment from the Chinese Wall Bridge past the old pumphouse towards the landing stage, to my left in the fading fields a

collection of black Nissen huts, and to my right, across the river, the mainland. As I was sitting on the breakwater waiting for the ferryman, the evening sun emerged from behind the clouds, bathing in its light the far-reaching arc of the seashore. The tide was advancing up the river, the water was shining like tinplate, and from the radio masts high above the marshes came an even, scarcely audible hum. The roofs and towers of Orford showed among the tree tops, seeming so close that I could touch them. There, I thought, I was once at home. And then, through the growing dazzle of the light in my eyes, I suddenly saw, amidst the darkening colours, the sails of the long-vanished windmills turning heavily in the wind.

# XI

# The Novelist, the Fisherman and the Prince

I n Rose Macaulay's novel *The World My Wilderness* the ruins of the City of London are the playground of two wild children, Barbary and her young half-brother Raul. One Sunday morning they discover in the rubble of a bombed church the charred pages of a prayer book, opened at the *Dies Irae*. Barbary chants the words in innocence: 'Day of wrath, O Day of Mourning! See fulfilled the prophet's warning, Heaven and earth in ashes burning!' Little Raul grows bored, so his sister places a stolen radio on the altar to listen to jazz. A strange priest stumbles through a window and, silencing the radio, hands the dumb-founded Barbary a censer. With a maddened stare he begins to perform Holy Communion but the words are those of Thomas Browne, 'Hell is where I am, Lucifer and all his legions are in me. Fire creeps on me from all sides . . . I cannot move my limbs, I cannot raise my hands to God. . . . The weight of my sins: they lie across my chest and pin me; I cannot stir. For this is hell, hell, hell.' The priest collapses when a second clergyman runs into the nave. He calms the terrified children, explaining that the priest wanders the ruined churches looking for his own, where for two days he was trapped in flaming wreckage.

For Rose Macaulay the Second World War seemed to

represent the end of civilisation and *The World My Wilderness* (1950) is the most nihilistic of her twenty novels, with quotations from *The Waste Land* inserted as a kind of fractured theme tune. When she read the poem on its publication in 1922 she admired Eliot's technical ability but at that time the words had no personal resonance for her. The world she found in 1945, however, seemed to be a fulfilment of Eliot's prophecies. In the final scene Barbary's elder brother Richie leaves the ruins and walks towards the shining dome of St Paul's. But this is a cynic's path to God, for Richie represents a disillusioned generation, a Cambridge undergraduate and a brave soldier who has become a black marketeer. His final words are Eliot's: 'I think we are in a rats' alley / Where the dead men lost their bones.'

Rose Macaulay wrote the book in her sixties. A member of Lord Macaulay's dynasty of liberal intellectuals, she was raised as a child of Nature in a beautiful villa on the coast of Italy, playing with the fishermen and learning to swim in the dangerous surf. When she was thirteen and her scholarly father returned to respectable society in Oxford, she horrified relatives with her bare feet, muddy knees and a tomboyish delight in tree-climbing. She never cared much for how she dressed: 'brownish' was the politest summary of her wardrobe. Impossibly thin – 'a jolly skeleton' – and impossibly spritely, she would dive into the Serpentine from the highest board at the age of seventy. In the 1930s her rusty bicycle chained to the railings of the London Library was one of the most familiar sights of literary London.

Without the tragedy of the war, Macaulay would be remembered for the earlier work for which she became popular: novels with an amusing eye for bossy aunts and shy curates, and accounts of travels in exotic scenery and as a familiar voice, tilted towards a Third Programme audience on tired afternoons. But during the Blitz she drove an ambulance, and night after night waited at the wheel while victims were pulled from burning wreckage. Then in July 1942, in Surrey, Gerald O'Donovan died of cancer. He had been her lover for more than twenty years, and they would have married if he had not been a Catholic and unwilling to leave his wife and three children. Her London flat was bombed, and although she was unharmed his letters perished in the flames. Many years later Macaulay's vigorous reaction was recalled as an inspiration by Natasha Spender, widow of Stephen, when her own house in France was destroyed by fire: 'I remember in the Blitz helping Rose Macaulay search the rubble of her bombed house where, as here, no treasure or mementos had survived. She seemed sensible, aloof from the drama, feelings of devastation in abeyance, a little dazed but taking refuge in activity.'

However detached she seemed, Macaulay wrote the jagged, raw 'Miss Anstruther's Letters', her most moving short story. In a few panicked moments after a bomb falls on her mansion block, its respectability now 'at one with Nineveh and Tyre', Miss Anstruther fills a suitcase with a typewriter, ornaments from the mantelpiece, and 'a walnut shell with tiny Mexicans behind glass'. At the bottom of the burning stairs she realises that she has forgotten her lover's letters – but the stairs are toppling, and the wardens bar her return. When the ashes grow cold all that remains of twenty-two years of love-letters is a single charred fragment, containing a jesting reproach. 'You don't care twopence, he seemed to say still; if you had cared twopence, you would have saved my letters, not your wireless and your typewriter and your china cow, least of all those little walnut Mexicans, which you know I never liked.' Why did only this reproach survive, not the letters about the steep hills in Devon, the balcony at the inn in Foix, the bedroom at Lisieux?

To research *The World My Wilderness* Macaulay became an explorer in the rubble of the City of London. Penelope Fitzgerald remembered the 'alarming experience' of scrambling after her, 'and keeping her spare form just in view as she shinned undaunted down a crater, or leaned, waving, through the smashed glass of some perilous window'. Macaulay described a bizarre new world:

> the great pits with their dense forests of bracken and
> bramble, golden ragwort and coltsfoot, fennel and
> foxglove and vetch, all the wild rambling shrubs that
> spring from ruin, the vaults and the cellars and caves, the
> wrecked guildhalls . . . the broken office stairways that
> spiralled steeply past empty doorways and rubbled
> closets into the sky, empty shells of churches with their
> towers still strangely spiring above the wilderness, their
> empty window arches where green boughs push in, their
> broken pavement floors . . . all this scarred and haunted
> green and stone and brambled wilderness lying under
> the August sun, a-hum with insects and astir with secret,
> darting, burrowing life, received the returning traveller
> into its dwellings with a wrecked, indifferent calm.

When she had explored the jungle of Guatemala for a travel book twenty years before, the Mayan temples slippery with vegetation had merely been Picturesque scenery. Now this new ruined landscape was the expression of 'an irremediable barbarism coming out of the earth, and of filth flung against the ivory tower'. The gutted City is the reflection of the inner wildness of her heroine Barbary, and of Macaulay's own nihilism. '"Where are the roots of that clutch, what branches grow, out of this stony rubbish? Son of man, you cannot say or guess. . . ." But you can say, you can guess, that it is yourself, your own roots, that clutch the stony rubbish, the branches of your own being that grow from it and nowhere else.' As *The Waste Land* had prophesied, below the respectable superstructure of society were 'the ruins of the soul; the shadowy dreams that lurked tenebrously in the cellars of consciousness; in the mysterious arcades and corridors and arcades of dreams, the wilderness that stretches not without but within'. By 1950 the craters and rubble were vanishing under a stratum of concrete, as new blocks of offices and houses rose. But the 'irredeemable barbarism' the ruins represented would rise to the surface elsewhere, for it was a spirit latent inside man.

Macaulay's mentor at this time was Professor Gilbert Murray, a distinguished classicist, who was convinced that Christian-Hellenic civilisation was an island in a 'sea of barbarism' represented by the Russians, Chinese and Arabs. Murray's son-in-law was Arnold Toynbee, who in his *History of the World*, published in ten volumes from 1934–54, analysed the cyclical rise and fall of civilisations. 'No civilisation had lasted for more than 1,000 years; this present one, called western culture, has had its day', says the cynical, well-read Richie in *The World My Wilderness*. But what came next?

What came next for Macaulay, at least, was a religious conversion which restored her faith in the future. An Anglican by birth but an agnostic for many decades, Macaulay converted to Catholicism at the age of seventy. The vigour of her irresistible *The Pleasure of Ruins* (1953) is the consequence of this late revival. For four years she read travellers' accounts of ruins, and became mesmerised by the images she discovered. She wrote to a friend: 'I am living in a ruinous world of crumbling walls, green jungle drowning temples and palaces in Mexico and Ceylon, friezes and broken columns sunk in the blue seas, with crabs scuttling about among them. Such dreams of beauty are haunting, like pleasure.'

The book is faulted by academics for the superficiality of its broad-brush picture of the cultures of the world. It is true, for example, that contrary to Macaulay's assurance the Romans did not paint ruins – at least to the best of my knowledge – and it is perhaps more interesting to understand this indifference than to assume they shared our enthusiasm. But this is to miss Macaulay's purpose. She wished to demonstrate the ubiquity of ruins in history in order to illustrate how in the eternal cycles of destruction and resurrection the goodness in man would always revive – and thus to reverse her own despondency in the face of the ruins of the Blitz. The final words of the book argued for the reconstruction of wholeness from the fragments of modernity:

> But Ruinenlust has come full circle: we have had our
> fill. . . . Ruin must be a fantasy, veiled by the mind's
> dark imaginings: in the objects that we see before us, we

get to agree with St Thomas Aquinas, that quae enim diminutae sunt, hoc ipso turpia sunt, and to feel that, in beauty, wholeness is all.

*The Pleasure of Ruins* is with John Harris's *No Voice from the Hall* and Lampedusa's *The Leopard* one of my three great inspirations. In Ladbroke Square, in West London, there is an apartment decorated with fragments of sculpture and ornament – and displayed with the same exhilaration as was shown by Soane – acquired by my friend Peter Hone in three Grand Tours to the sites described in *The Pleasure of Ruins*. In the 1960s he travelled to the Middle East in a Volkswagen van, accompanied by an Abyssinian princess named Marie White who had been a model for Jacob Epstein and now worked in Peter's antique shop in Islington. At Mount Olympus he burned a copy of Macaulay's book as a sacrifice; at Palmyra they parked the Volkswagen for two weeks in the shadow of the colonnades; at Ephesus Marie stayed in the van while Peter slept inside a cave.

One of the most significant journeys to ruins in modern times was John Harris's exploration of Britain in the years after the Second World War. Today Harris has written more academic articles on historic country houses and curated more exhibitions than any architectural historian in Britain. Having him as a guide to the English landscape is like peering at aerial photographs in which patterns below the surface become visible: as he speaks, a vanished England arises, with country houses, canals and garden statues appearing as ghostly, sepia-grey mirages in cornfields, golf-courses and housing estates. But at the end of the war he was

Marie White, pictured in the ruins of Baalbec in the 1960s, on the journey with Peter Hone inspired by Rose Macaulay's *Pleasure of Ruins*.

fifteen years old, a truculent boy who had left his apprenticeship. In 1945 the ornamental canals at country houses were filled with fish fattened after six years without disturbance. He visited them on fishing expeditions with his uncle Sid, who was also a buyer at country house auctions.

The first his nephew attended was at Langley Park, near Slough, which had once belonged to Sir Robert Grenville Harvey, a big-game hunter in India who also spied for Queen Victoria on the Northwest Frontier. Leaving the chatter of the auction Harris found a derelict orangery which, he discovered, contained Harvey's museum of stuffed animal heads: the door had not been opened for many years, and he fainted at the stench of decaying fur. In the garden at Langley Harvey had erected a column in the Anglo-Indian style, from the top of which you could see Windsor Castle. It had survived target practice from Polish soldiers training for D-day, only to be blown up by the Modernist county planning officer a few years later. Only later did Sid and his nephew discover that the lake in which they stopped to fish was filled with discarded phosphorus bombs.

Harris had discovered a world in limbo. In Britain two thousand country houses – almost every one of any architectural value – had been requisitioned by the military six years before. Now the soldiers had gone, and their owners returned to find Nissen huts rusting on the lawn, avenues of trees felled, family portraits used as dart-boards and garden temples as targets for mortar practice. It was a dispiriting sight, and many families threw in their hand in despair. Harris could soon spot the tell-tale signs of an abandoned estate:

> Estate care has been abandoned within the park
> perimeter, the hedgerows are unkempt. A clear divide is
> discernible at the gate or lodge between the public road
> and the drive across the park: on one side maintenance,

on the other decay. The lodge might be shut up, the
gates locked. The drive is crumbling, often weeded
over. A decayed park in late spring or summer, the
parkland ungrazed, colourful with wild flowers, the
lawns unmown and garden divisions returned to nature:
so many of my houses appear to me in this floral frame.
. . . Watch for broken windows, scattering of rubbish:
both are good signs for the country-house prowler. At
this juncture the house always seems to be cocooned in
a pressing silence. There is a blankness in its glassy stare.

These houses were in a state of suspension, awaiting either
a reprieve or an execution by owners who did not have the
resources, or the inclination, to repair them. On the dole,
Harris travelled to more than two hundred derelict
mansions. He slept in youth hostels – indeed, he was
awarded the prize for the most hostels visited in one year –
and in barns when necessary, and once in a deserted church
lying wrapped in scented cassocks. Of the mansions he
visited personally, three-quarters were subsequently demolished. In 1955, at the height of the destruction, two
country houses were demolished each week. This was the
greatest loss to British architecture since the Dissolution of
the monasteries, far greater in aesthetic value than the
damage caused by German bombs.

Saddest of all was Burwell in Lincolnshire, a perfect
Georgian doll's house. Harris visited it in 1957, by which
time he travelled on a Lambretta as a paid fieldworker for
Pevsner's *Buildings of England* series. A knock at the
entrance met with a strange shuffling inside; opening the
door, he was tumbled off his feet by a flock of sheep. They

Sacks of potatoes in the drawing-room at Burwell in Lincolnshire, as discovered by John Harris in 1957. The following year the mansion was demolished.

had been penned in the staircase hall, below cobwebbed portraits of the family, by the local farmer. Amid Burwell's interiors of rococo plasterwork, not updated since the house was built in the 1760s, were sacks of potatoes in the drawing-room, and heaps of grain in the saloon. The following year he received a telephone call announcing Burwell's demolition, and the rush to the scene of destruction reminds us of Piper's journeys during the Blitz. The roof and walls were gone, and clouds of soft, powdering plaster rose as men hacked at the decorations with pickaxes. Black with rage and despair, all Harris could do was to rescue six plaster heads from the debris – like William Stukeley collecting fragments of stained glass and sculpture all those years before. The preservation of country houses in the 1950s seemed as futile as the protection of medieval architecture had been in the 1720s, but Harris's journey was to be as significant as the rediscovery of the neglected castles and abbeys by the generation of Stukeley and Dyer.

The photograph on the cover of Harris's memoir, *No Voice from the Hall* (1998) shows a hand touching an ivy-mantled portico; peer closely, and you will see that the cuff and buttons have been removed. He tears away all his shirt-collars too, unable to bear constriction, and a full-length photograph would show eyebrows as stiff as horse-hair, and a red face so vital with the promise of discovery that it is easy to understand why so many strangers opened their doors to the boy.

While the war was still in progress, Osbert Sitwell had employed John Piper to paint views of his family mansion, Renishaw Hall in Derbyshire, in the conviction that the end of the country house was inevitable. In visits over the three years 1942–4 Piper painted more than fifty views of the gaunt Georgian house and its desolate temples, lodges and woodland. Sitwell's commission was integral to the writing of his autobiography, *Left Hand, Right Hand*: Piper's paintings were stacked three-deep in his study, an inspirational version of a writer's card-index. When the series was exhibited in January 1945, Sitwell introduced the catalogue:

> At the very moment when the great English houses, the
> chief architectural expression of their country, are
> passing, being wrecked by happy and eager planners, or
> becoming the sterilised and scionless possessions of the

National Trust, a painter has appeared to hand them on
to future ages, as Canaletto or Guardí handed on the
dying Venice of their day, and with an equally
inimitable art. And so it was to this painter, Mr John
Piper, that I turned when I began my autobiography for
in that book I was trying to record a way of life, as well
as my own adventures, in my own medium.

Harris was more vigorous than Sitwell, however, and
over the next decades was the leading figure in the nascent
movement to rescue our country houses. The turn in the
tide of public opinion and of government action did not
come until 1974, when Harris and Marcus Binney
organised the *Destruction of the Country House* exhibition
at the Victoria and Albert Museum. The whole exhibition
was designed as a ruin, with photographs of demolished
houses pasted on to cubes of rubble. In the spot-lit
darkness the gruff voice of Harris recounted their names,
as if a litany of the fallen: Gopsall, Stratton, Kempshott,
Slindon, Richings, Burwell, Willingham, Iver, Staunton. . . .
Today the good cause has triumphed, thanks in large part
to the truant fisherman who fell under the spell of this
magical kingdom of ruins. But as with the abbeys and the
antiquaries, brutal destruction was the necessary prelude to
appreciation.

But the greatest example of the perverse fertility of ruin,
and of how genius germinates in architectural decay, was the
Prince of Lampedusa, author of *The Leopard*. His ancestral
palace in Palermo was destroyed by American bombs in the
invasion of Sicily in 1943. The last prince, in a line of many
centuries, Giuseppe Tomasi di Lampedusa, had been born

in the palace in 1896, and slept in the same room almost up to '5th April 1943, the day on which bombs brought from beyond the Atlantic searched her out and destroyed her'. After Lampedusa discovered the 'repugnant ruins', he walked in a state of shock 8 miles to a friend's house where he sat without speaking, and covered in dust, for three days. When he died in 1957, to contemporaries in Palermo his life seemed to have been as gilded, dusty and idle as an elegant old wardrobe – but no one knew that the wardrobe contained the manuscript of what is the finest Italian novel of the twentieth century, and perhaps the finest in post-war Europe.

Lampedusa wrote *The Leopard* in the last two years of his life, during which time he also wrote a memoir, *Places of My Infancy*, which was never intended for publication but as an exercise to neutralise his nostalgia. His childhood had been paradise, he recalled. The only son, he was the ruler of three courtyards, staircases and stables. The façade of the Baroque palace ran along the street for 70 yards, and its destruction revealed in rubble a floor area 1,600 square yards in extent. This home was a 'Beloved':

> I loved [it] with utter abandon, and still love it now when for the last twelve years it has been no more than a memory. Until a few months before its destruction I used to sleep in the room where my mother's bed had stood when she gave me birth. And in that house, in that very room maybe, I was glad to feel a certainty of dying.

The intense sunlight of Sicily streamed into the row of

drawing-rooms behind the façade, diluted by the silk blinds on the nine balconies, or reflected on gilt furniture; when the shutters were closed at the height of summer, a single ray was

> populated with myriads of dust particles, and going to vilify the colours of carpets, uniformly ruby-red throughout all the drawing-rooms: a real sorcery of illumination and colour which entranced my mind for ever. Sometimes I rediscover this luminous quality in some old palace or church, and it would wrench at my heart were I not ready to brush it aside with some 'wicked joke'.

At the turn of the century Palermo was a fashionable resort for European royalty, and his earliest memories were of being presented to the Empress Eugénie of France, or of eating ice-creams inside a liveried carriage parked outside a café; it was considered vulgar to sit at a table. Later, Lampedusa realised that such elegance was the final indulgence of an aristocracy which had been in decline since the abolition of feudalism in Sicily in 1812. Only 20 of the 200 aristocratic palaces in Palermo were in use, and his family were particularly short of money; by the 1920s they were forced to let a wing of the palace to the municipal gas board. Giuseppe's great-grandfather had died suddenly of cholera in 1885 without leaving a will, and the inheritance was disputed by nine children and their squabbling descendants. Giuseppe was heir to the title but to only one-fiftieth of the patrimony.

The idleness of the family is astonishing to northerners, as described in David Gilmour's superlative biography of the writer. His father was dilatory and self-indulgent, as were three of Lampedusa's four paternal uncles; the fourth was a distinguished diplomat and boasted of being the first Lampedusa in a thousand years to have a job. He was also the last, Gilmour observes. After fighting bravely in the First World War, Giuseppe decided not to pursue a profession or to earn a living, or indeed to take any action to reverse the family's decline into ruin. In the 1920s he travelled and after marrying a German baroness in 1932 divided his time between her castle in Latvia and his palace in Palermo; Licy refused to sleep in a room next to his mother, but Giuseppe would not leave his mother's side. After the American bombing of Palermo the majority of displaced aristocrats moved into new apartments outside the centre but Giuseppe and Licy – unable to return home, her castle seized by the Soviets – moved deeper into the bomb-damaged historic core. From the balcony of No. 42 Via Butera they were entertained by the sight of prostitutes enticing clients into the debris. In No. 42's library Giuseppe installed a mantelpiece rescued from the palace, and doors and windows salvaged from ruined buildings in the neighbourhood.

In the years after the war he would leave Via Butera for breakfast at Pasticceria del Massimo, where he would eat pastries and read for four hours – enough time for a Balzac novel. Then he visited the bookseller Flaccovio. His bulky leather bag, full of books and cream cakes, was always at his side. He never left the house without a copy of Shakespeare, noted Licy, and Flaccovio once glimpsed Proust nestling in courgettes. In the afternoon he joined a table of local intellectuals at Café Caflisch, silent but for the occasional monosyllabic retort. A shabby but distinctive figure, he was 'tall, stout, and silent, a pale face – that greyish pallor of dark-skinned southerners', remembered the novelist Giorgio Bassani.

After many years of this routine Lampedusa was overweight, pale and one of the best-read men in Europe. In 1955 he abandoned the Caflisch circle for the Café Mazzara where, at the base of a modern tower block, he wrote in blue biro every afternoon for the last thirty months of his life. There were two triggers for such a sudden change after a lifetime of passive inactivity. First, he had accompanied his cousin Lucio Piccolo to collect a prize for his poetry at a literary festival – where Bassani had encountered him – and realised he could do better than any of the literati assembled there. Second, he agreed to teach some young students English literature, and therefore began to analyse and synthesise a lifetime of reading. These were only catalysts, however. The destruction of the palace had made him realise that a world was vanishing without any record. As the novel's hero reflects on his death-bed, facing the same marine drive as did No. 42 Via Butera: 'the significance of a noble family lies entirely in its traditions, that is in its vital memories; and he was the last to have any unusual memories, anything different from those of other families'.

The novel began as twenty-four hours in the life of the Prince of Salina during Garibaldi's invasion of Sicily in 1860. Like the Prince of Lampedusa in 1860 – the greatgrandfather who never made a will – Salina is an astronomer and the father of many children. His physical impressiveness is Giuseppe's romantic projection, however, and as he describes his hero shaving and dressing he seems to be

infatuated by his own creation: '*Mio Principone*,' whispers
Salina's grateful mistress, while the family and the retainers
are in awe of the graceful giant who bends coins with his
fingers. What the writer gave the Prince was his own
intelligence and introspection. And like Lampedusa the
Leopard scorns his own decadent class, but sees no virtue in
the new government. His only consolation is in the eternal
certainties of the stars.

What is so compelling to the reader from the north is the
passive resignation of the virile, perceptive Prince to a
process of destructive change; it is the same puzzle as why
for decades Lucio Piccolo did not bother to send his poems
to a publisher, or why the Palazzo Lampedusa is still a bomb
site today. It is the mentality of an island in which the
shadow of the past stultifies the activity of the present.

The apparent subject of the novel was the Risorgimento,
and how the hopes of reform raised by Garibaldi's red-shirts
were frustrated by the cynical politicians of the united Italy.
But this was only the repetition of a pattern which had been
recurring for two millennia, in which Sicily had been
invaded and conquered by Greeks, Carthaginians, Romans,
Goths, Arabs, Normans and Spaniards. Each time the
islanders' hopes had been disappointed, and now they had
no faith in promises of future improvement. Salina explains
to an envoy from the new government in Turin:

> For over twenty-five centuries we've been bearing the
> weight of superb and heterogenous civilisations, all from
> outside, none made by ourselves, none that we could
> call our own. . . . Sleep, my dear Chevalley, sleep, that is
> what Sicilians want, and they will always hate anyone

who tries to wake them, even in order to bring them the
most wonderful of gifts.

Lampedusa believed that modern Sicily was irredeemable
– and yet he loved a romantic idea of the island which is
explained in a short story, 'The Professor and the Siren', also
written in those final months. In a café in Milan a young
libertine befriends a fellow *émigré* from Sicily, the great
scholar of the Hellenistic world Professor La Ciura. The
Professor is persuaded to reveal his deepest secret by their
shared memories of Sicily – memories of 'eternal Sicily,
nature's Sicily; about the scent of rosemary on the Nebrodi
hills, the taste of Melilli, the waving corn seen from Etna on
a windy day in May, of the solitudes around Syracuse, the
gusts of scent from orange and lemon groves pouring over
Palermo, it's said, during some sunsets in June'. As a young
student fifty years before, in a rocky bay of the sea which had
not changed since it was sighted by Grecian mariners, La
Ciura was seduced by a mermaid. The romance combined
the primitiveness of a satyr with the eternity of the stars, for
the Siren had loved Greeks, and Romans, and Normans, and
Spaniards in the twenty-five centuries of her existence.
When, at sea, the Professor disappears overboard, the young
man understands that he has returned to the Siren. In the
Professor's will he receives a Greek vase painted with Siren
figures, but during the war it is destroyed by a bomb. If the
Siren is Sicily in her tanned, languid, laughing-eyed and
immortal beauty, the scornful but intense old man is
Lampedusa.

Lampedusa finished *The Leopard* in August 1956, but
received rejections from a series of publishers who believed

that all modern Italian novels should be 'progressive' and 'committed to the future'. The final rejection was on 17 July when he was in a clinic suffering from lung cancer; six days later he was dead. The exercise book in blue biro was filed away by his widow.

On 3 March 1958 she received a call from Giorgio Bassani, who advised the publisher Feltrinelli and was later to write *The Garden of the Finzi-Continis*, a novel which – in part inspired by the gardens of Ninfa – also showed how the past can be a more vivid presence than the future. Bassani had received a spare typescript of the manuscript which had been posted to a friend in Rome more than twelve months before. The friend had left the package on the shelf of a porter's lodge, before passing it to Bassani. From the very first pages, he now told Licy, he recognised the hand of a great writer. Unfortunately, Licy told him, the writer had recently died. *The Leopard* was published in November 1958, and by the following March – just five months later – had been reprinted fifty-two times. 'One of the great novels of this century,' wrote the French intellectual Louis Aragon in his review, 'one of the great novels of all time.'

One summer I retraced the Leopard's steps, and at the end of this journey I realised that although Lampedusa intended his novel to be a memorial to a world which had vanished he had inadvertently created a new and vivid world in its ruins. It was a lesson all the more compelling in an island which is littered by the ruins of fallen civilisations.

Palazzo Lampedusa in Palermo remains in rubble, and amid the debris of the city centre the many palaces which do still survive resemble the ruins of Rome in the Dark Ages: washing lines are strung between marble columns in their courtyards, and families crowd into cellars and ballrooms partitioned by corrugated iron. Lampedusa's family also owned four palaces in the Sicilian countryside, and today every one is derelict, crumbling, or destroyed. In 1955 Lampedusa travelled south in search of 'vital memories' to the palaces of Sta Margherita la Belice and Palma di Montechiaro, which in the novel became fused into the 'Donnafugata' where Tancredi meets the exquisite Angelica – they were played in Visconti's film of 1966 by Alain Delon and Claudia Cardinale. I followed his route over the 'lovely and desperately sad landscape' of central Sicily, with a growing sense of the timelessness – of progress suspended, of the dead outnumbering the living – which is so disconcerting yet liberating to an Englishman. At Agrigento are the colossal Doric temples whose ruins warned the young John Soane of the futility of trying to rival the ancients; between their columns you now see the tower blocks of the poorest city in Italy and a motorway raised on concrete stilts. Almond trees fill the valley between the two. When the Greeks erected the temples in the fifth century BC, when the Siren was already old, the city had a population of two hundred thousand and its walls contained an inhabited area larger than that of the deserted valley.

Palma di Montechiaro also seems to illustrate Lampedusa's conclusion that Sicily was irredeemable, whatever the possibilities of technological progress. The town was founded by a pious Saint-Duke of Lampedusa in 1637 as a 'New Jerusalem', with a cathedral and palace on a central piazza. The vast palace is a derelict, barred shell today, surrounded by modern concrete houses, many of which are half-built; it is a custom for each generation to build one storey and when a house terminates in a frame of rusty steel rods it is a sign that the children have moved away. The piazza was deserted, except for a priest walking his dog – until a tall, bare-shouldered man loped across the square. 'Get away,' whispered the priest to me, 'this man is dangerous.' As we returned to the car the thug loomed over Anna and me, muttering obscenities in dialect as we refused to accept his invitation of a guided tour; rarely have I been so grateful for the sound of an ignition key. We fled the New Jerusalem, and a menace which was all the more terrifying because it seemed to have no spectators. Not a soul had stirred in the sleeping, dead-eyed town.

Sta Margherita la Belice was a happier place, a town on a hilltop with a faint but welcome breeze; there is even a little neo-classical rotunda built during the Napoleonic Wars so that English officers could enjoy the prospect. Until debts forced the sale of the palace in 1921 Giuseppe came here for summer holidays. After a journey of twelve parched, dusty hours the family would be greeted by the mayor and the municipal band playing a polka.

Sta Margherita was shattered by the 1968 earthquake – the same earthquake which destroyed Ghibellina – but there was a vivacity in the newly built streets, with children skipping to the café in the piazza for ice-cream. Its name 'Il Gattopardo' is the town's only dedication to Lampedusa, and the palace is in ruins. Only the Baroque façade withstood the earthquake, and the attached church was split in two as perfectly as an anatomical section. This is Sicily, and it is as if the earthquake happened yesterday: the hoardings declaring IN RESTORATION are covered with dust, and no mould or moss grows in the dry heat.

With *Places of My Infancy* in my hand – and with the Prince, Tancredi and Angelica in mind – I walked under the Baroque portico into a wilderness where there had once been a hundred rooms around three courtyards. Only two or three rooms survived. Its chambers were 'a kind of 18th-century Pompeii . . . I was a boy who loved solitude, who liked the company of things more than people. . . . I would wander through the vast ornate house as in an enchanted wood.' Each new room was like a sunlit clearing, light

Sta Margherita La Belice before the earthquake. Prince Giuseppe Tomasi di Lampedusa spent his childhood summers in the palace of Sta Margherita La Belice in Sicily, and it inspired Donnafugata in his novel, *The Leopard*.

flickering on the portraits of ancestors, silk hangings, and with monkeys and flowers weaving through the tapestries. The rooms led into a private balcony overlooking the altar of the church, where the family sat for Mass, and the boy peered through the flowering gilt railing. Astonishingly, the balcony he described survives, clinging to the high wall of the ruin as a precarious, rusted relic of the little prince.

Lampedusa once remarked that if Europe was destroyed by a hydrogen bomb, London would be immortal in the novels of Dickens but Palermo would disappear because not a single good writer had recorded the city on paper. That was before he began to write. Sta Margherita, I realised – and indeed I began to smile – is more vivid as a ruin which can be explored with Lampedusa's writings to hand than if it had survived intact. In the garden which had been a 'paradise of parched scents' palm-trees stand tilted by the earthquake and surrounded by thistles. The flight of stairs is there; there, the thicket of bamboo; the fountain in which a nude goddess was courted by tritons and nereids spurting water. The statues have gone, as have the dolls' house, and the monkey cage. But spring-water still gurgles into the basin of the siren's fountain, and with the scent of ragged flowers, and the dusty rays of sunlight streaming through the ruined walls, Sta Margherita is tenderly but ecstatically alive. I had finished the journey.

Anna is sitting by the fountain, eating an ice-cream. 'Let's go to the beach,' she says, without urgency. 'It would be nice to have a swim.' It was time to leave the ruins.

# Acknowledgements

I must thank all the owners of ruins who did not set their dogs on me when I trespassed – and, in particular, the unknown owner of the Priory at Winchelsea in Sussex. On a downcast spring day I walked over the marshes from Rye and stumbled across this roofless church. Its arches were full of marigolds, and a child's swing creaked under an adjacent apple tree.

In writing this book my inspiration was Charles Sprawson's book on the exhilaration of swimming in rivers and lakes, *The Haunts of the Black Masseur*. Charles's masterly study of swimmers in history reminds modern society of a pleasure it has lost; it is not a manual on 'how to swim' or how to manage modern leisure centres. Similarly, my book is not intended to address the practical issues of how to open archaeological sites to the public but, rather, to show what a source of inspiration ruins have been in earlier centuries. Whether or not readers agree with my views is less important than if this book reminds them of their own enjoyment of ruins.

Jenny Uglow of Chatto & Windus suggested I write the book, and the most rewarding aspect has been to discover writers whom I might otherwise have never read: John Dyer, John Clare, Ferdinand Gregorovius, Giorgio Bassani, and others. The greatest treat has been an excuse to read the ten volumes of Chateaubriand's *Mémoires de l'outre-tombe*, which is in my view – a view founded on no authority whatsoever – the greatest autobiography ever written. Its 1902 translation by Alexander Teixera de Mattos is an irreplaceable work of scholarship; we can survive without the passages he omitted as containing 'a little too much of the *esprit gaulois* to English taste'.

I began the book as a straightforward architectural historian but soon realised that architects were twenty years behind painters in their thinking – and that painters in turn took their ideas from writers. I finished, therefore, as an enthusiastic but sophomoric student of English Literature, and am particularly grateful to David Skilton, Professor at Cardiff, and Andrew Sanders, at Durham, for their guidance.

Among my friends who are architectural historians, the two to whom I am deeply indebted are Roger Bowdler and Jeremy Musson – each of whom could have written this book if they had not been busy fathering children. Roger and I met at the National Gallery one evening and he suggested we choose 'ruins in paintings' as the theme for our stroll around; he explained to me the relationship of stone, flesh, and moss; later, he introduced me to grisly but wonderful peculiarities such as the Tradescants' tomb in the churchyard at Lambeth. Jeremy Musson at *Country Life* gave me a stream of ideas scribbled on postcards, a treasured first edition of Rose Macaulay's *The World My Wilderness* and, above all, the assurance that he would be interested in what I discovered. Jenifer Cargill-Thompson suggested Wheeler's lines, used as the epigraph. Of course, I would never have had the privilege of being an architectural historian if David Watkin had not gracefully accepted me on to his course at Cambridge after I stumbled into the History of Art Faculty during one dishevelled May Week.

Finally, I must thank my wife Anna, who married me on the Campidoglio last summer: the Registry office is in Michelangelo's piazza on the Capitoline Hill, overlooking the Forum. A Roman of slender, perfect and timeless symmetry, she rescued me from libraries, graveyards, 'dead stones'. *Sono molto fiero che mio figlio sarà mezzo-Romano.*

# Illustrations

*Endpapers*: aerial cutaway view of the Bank of England drawn by Joseph Michael Gandy, architect Sir John Soane, reproduced by courtesy of the Trustees of Sir John Soane's Museum, London.

The author and publishers are grateful to all the individuals and institutions who have kindly granted permission for the reproduction of illustrations, as noted in the above list.

# Notes

The place of publication is London, unless otherwise stated.

I *Who Killed Daisy Miller?*

Michiel Sweerts is one of the most enigmatic and admired Dutch painters of the seventeenth century, the subject of several studies by Rolf Kultzen. Born in Brussels in 1618, his training as an artist remains a mystery but by 1646 he was recorded as living in Rome; on his return from Brussels in 1656 he opened a life-drawing academy and at the same time began to reveal his religious fanaticism; it is this, I imagine, which explains the painting in the Rijksmuseum. Sweerts joined a party of Catholic missionaries travelling through Syria to the Far East, and he died in Goa in 1664.

For the disappearance of classical Rome, the *disabitato*, and the appearance of the ruins to Christian pilgrims in the early Middle Ages, see Richard Krautheimer, *Rome: Profile of a City, 312–1308* (New Jersey, 1980). Rodolfo Lanciani (1847–1929) drew his conclusions in *The Destruction of Ancient Rome* (1906) and his letters to the fine arts journal *The Athenaeum* were published as *Notes from Rome*, edited by Anthony L. Cubberley (British School at Rome, 1988). These are the best eye-witness accounts of excavation in the years after unification; Lanciani was one of the leading archaeologists of the period, but had an eye to the

Picturesque beauties which have since disappeared. *The Eagle and the Spade* by Ronald Ridley (Cambridge, 1992) is a vivid study of the first systematic excavations in the Forum, those made during the Napoleonic occupation of Rome from 1809–14. Ridley (p. 141) describes the French plan of 1812 to turn the Forum into an 'English garden', referred to in Chapter Six.

For a narrative of visitors' reactions to the Colosseum in visitors' eyes, see Peter Quenell, *The Colosseum* (London and New York, 1973), which also includes an anthology of their descriptions; for a study of its design, G. Cozzo, *The Colosseum* (Rome, 1971).

Among the biographies of Edgar Allan Poe the best analysis of the poem 'The Coliseum' and its relationship to *Politian* and *MS Found in a Bottle* is Kenneth Silverman (*Edgar Allan Poe*, 1992), pp. 92, 115. The letter to a friend relating to 'man's advance towards perfection' written in 1844 is quoted in Jeffrey Meyers, *Edgar A. Poe* (1992), p. 293, as are D. H. Lawrence's observations on the author. Meyers discusses the background to *Politian* (p. 77), extracts from which Poe published after his appointment as editor of the *Southern Literary Messenger* in December 1835.

Chateaubriand published the final volume of *Mémoires d'outre-tombe* in 1850, and it was translated into English by Alexander Teixera de Mattos in 1902 (Freemantle).

Alex Scobie's definitive book *Hitler's State Architecture* (Philadelphia, 1990) studies all aspects of the dictator's interest in classical architecture, and reveals his obsession with ruins.

Doré's image of the New Zealander appeared in *London*,

a book of his views of the modern city published in 1872 and accompanied by text by Blanchard Ferrold. The metaphor was conceived by Thomas Macaulay in his review of Von Ranke's *History of the Papacy* published in *The Edinburgh Review*, October 1840.

II *A Perverse Pleasure*
For the aqueducts, see *The Waters of Rome* by H. V. Morton (1966). Beckford's descriptions of Rome are in *Dreams, Waking Thoughts and Incidents*, a travel book which he published in 1779 but soon after suppressed; Robert Gemmett edited a version (New Jersey, 1971).

III *Haunted Houses*
The poem of the soldier's return is translated by Arthur Waley in *170 Chinese Poems* (London, 1923). Several of the poems chosen by Waley have ruins as their subject and he notes that by the T'ang dynasty (618–905 AD) the re-visiting of a ruined city or old home is an established literary trope.

Emily Ruete, Princess Salme of Zanzibar and Oman, wrote her *Memoirs of an Arabian Princess from Zanzibar* in German; a translation was recently published by the eccentric and wonderful Gallery bookshop in Stone Town, Zanzibar.

The best study of Byron at Newstead aside from Leslie Marchand's standard biography of 1971 is the catalogue edited by Haidee Jackson for the exhibition held at Newstead Abbey in 1998, 'Ruinous Perfection'.

IV *Ephesus without an Umbrella*
Richard Holmes's study of the Baths of Caracalla and

*Prometheus Unbound* is in *Shelley: The Pursuit* (1974), pp. 489–509.

Flaubert's letter on Thebes was written to Louis Bouilhet on 2 June 1850 and is published in *Selected Letters*, ed. Geoffrey Wall (Harmondsworth, 1997), p. 149.

The rebuilding of Noto is the subject of an excellent book by Stephen Tobriner (1982).

*The Roman Journals of Ferdinand Gregorovius* (1821–91) were translated into English by Mrs Gustavus Hamilton in 1911.

## V *An Exemplary Frailty*

The relationship between architectural decay and human mortality is analysed by Dr Roger Bowdler in 'A Sad Prospect to the Soul' in *The Cult of the Ruin*, the Proceedings of the Georgian Group Symposium of 1998 (2001: to be published). The discussion of the seventeenth century is based on Bowdler's work.

The Tate's picture of Hadleigh Castle is a full-size sketch, and the final version which he exhibited at the Royal Academy is in the Paul Mellon Center for British Art, Connecticut. The episode is described in *The Later Paintings and Drawings of John Constable* by Graham Reynolds (Yale, 1984), pp. 199–202. The castle is on the Thames shore, near Southend-on-Sea.

For Walter Scott and Williamina Forbes I paraphrase A. N. Wilson, *A Life of Walter Scott* (1996 edn.), pp. 60–64.

## VI *Time's Shipwreck*

*Goths and Vandals* by M. S. Briggs (1952) remains the best overview on how attitudes to medieval buildings have changed in the centuries since their Dissolution, and is particularly vivid on the sixteenth century; he quotes the letter from Lewes.

It would be tedious to list all the examples from which I tried to construct a composite, but I would mention a few. John Aislabie of Studley Royal also built a house overlooking the ruins of Waverley Abbey, Surrey, which he landscaped, and he collaborated with John Vanbrugh on the campaign to save the Holbein Arch on Whitehall (see C. Woodward, 'A Pre-History of Conservation', in *Transactions of the Society for Studies in the Conservation of Historic Buildings*, 1995). Rev. William Gilpin found the gable ends of Tintern Abbey too 'regular' and suggested that a 'mallet judiciously used (but who durst use it?) might be of service in fracturing them'. This was not done, although the stone pulpitum across the nave was removed in the nineteenth century in order to open the vista. The only examples of the smashing of window tracery in order to enhance a vista are at Guisborough Priory and Kenilworth Castle: see Joe Mordaunt Crook's introduction to the reprint (Leicester, 1970) of Charles Lock Eastlake, *A History of the Gothic Revival*, 1872. Examples of the re-erection of Gothic ruins are at Shobdon in Herefordshire, and the removal of pieces of Netley Abbey to Cranbury Park in Hampshire (see C. Woodward, 'Ruins as Follies', *Country Life*, 8 October 1998).

*Great Romantic Ruins of England and Wales* by Brian Bailey (New York, 1984) is a gazetteer of historic ruins of all types, including abbeys, illustrated with excellent photographs by his wife Rita. For a thorough study of twentieth-century attitudes to the preservation of ruins by archaeologists, see Gill Chitty, 'A Prospect of Ruins' in

*Transactions of the Society for Studies in the History of Conservation*, 1993, pp. 43–60.

There are many books on eighteenth-century gardens but the most eloquent and incisive overviews are *The Picturesque* by David Watkin (1982) and Mavis Batey and David Lambert, *The English Garden Tour* (1990). Watkin explains the fictive way of seeing, Batey and Lambert the visitors' participation in its delights.

Sir John Vanbrugh's letter is transcribed in *The Complete Works of Sir John Vanbrugh*, ed. Geoffrey Webb (1928), pp. 29–30. For a brief account of the Woodstock Manor episode, see *The Work of John Vanbrugh* by Geoffrey Beard (1986), pp. 37–50.

There is a literary analysis of John Dyer and a succinct biography in Belinda Humphrey, *John Dyer* (Cardiff, 1980). *Grongar Hill* was reprinted by Stourton Press in 1983 with illustrations by John Piper.

The best single studies of individual ruins are of the folly at Fawley Court by Geoffrey Tyack (*Country Life*, 20 April 1989) and by David Adshead, 'The Design and Building of the Gothic Folly at Wimpole, Cambridgeshire' in *The Burlington Magazine*, February 1998, pp. 76–83. The suggestion that the latter castle was built to celebrate the fall of a 'Gothic' political order was made by David Stewart in *The Journal of the Society of Architectural Historians of America* (1997).

The Rev. Clubbe as antiquarian and wit is the subject of 'John Clubbe and the Antiquities of Wheatfield' by Alison Shell in *The Book Trade and its Customers 1450–1900*, ed. Arnold Hunt (Winchester, 1997). Stuart Piggott wrote the biography of William Stukeley (2nd edn., 1985).

Bacon's metaphor of 'Time's Shipwreck' is in *Advancement of Learning*, II, section 1. The metaphor is that of Vossius in *De philologia liber*, 'Antiquities are the remains of ancient times, similar to the debris of a shipwreck'.

For the Jealous Wall at Belvedere see the chapter on 'Ruins and Eye-Catchers' in *The Follies and Garden Buildings of Ireland* by James Howley (New Haven, 1993), and *Titles* by Leo Daley (1981), pp. 42–67, for an accurate account of the scandal.

## VII *Serious Follies*

Virginia Water is studied in Jane Roberts, *Royal Landscape: The Gardens and Parks at Windsor* (New Haven and London, 1997), pp. 457–61, and the most detailed study of the stones from the archaeological point of view is by G. E. Chambers, 'The "Ruins" at Virginia Water' in the *Journal of the Berkshire Archaeological Society*, 1953–4.

The catalogue of an exhibition, *Visions of Ruin*, which I curated at Sir John Soane's Museum in 1999, with essays by David Watkin, Helen Dorey and myself, studied English 'follies' in greater detail.

The artificial ruin in the Duke of Urbino's park at Pesaro – long vanished – is described and illustrated in Antonio Pinelli and Orietta Rossi, *Genga Architetto* (Rome, 1971), pp. 246–51. The unexecuted project of *c*.1730 for the backdrop to the Trevi Fountain is recorded in a drawing in the Kunstbibliothek, Berlin, reproduced in Bruce Boucher, *Italian Baroque Sculpture* (1998), p. 107.

The ruin room at Sta Trinità dei Monti is on pp. 103–12 of Thomas McCormick's monograph on the artist, *Charles-*

*Louis Clérisseau and the Genesis of Neo-Classicism* (Cambridge, Mass., and London, 1990).

William Chambers was the subject of a monograph by John Harris (London, 1970), and the mausoleum for the Prince of Wales and the Kew Gardens are discussed on pp. 23–4 and 32–9.

For German follies, including Schloss Löwenburg, see Günter Hartmann, *Die Ruine im Landschaftsgarten* (Worms, 1981).

The late Jean de Cayeux was the authority on Hubert Robert, on whom there is no good study in English; his daughter Mme Roland Michel has the archive at her gallery in Paris and is the continuing expert on dating his pictures. De Cayeux's biography (1989) is published by Fayard, and in 1987 he studied Robert's complex role in the design and recording of Picturesque gardens in *Hubert Robert et les Jardins* (Editions Herscher), a book which also describes Ermenonville and illustrates the garden of the Petits-Augustin. The Musée de Valence has a great holding of Robert's work, and in 1989 they studied his enigmatic response to the Revolution: *Hubert Robert et la Révolution* (Valence, 1989). Marie-Catherine Sahut curated the exhibition *Le Louvre du Hubert Robert* (Paris, 1979), which is the definitive discussion of the 'Louvre in Ruins' pictures. Mlle Stephanie Thuilliez is writing a PhD on Robert at the Sorbonne which will explore these ideas further, as in her article 'La poétique de la variété: les ruines et la terre' in *Bulletin de l'Association des Historiens de l'Art Italien* (Paris, 1996). Diderot's review of the Salon of 1767 is published in Diderot, *Salons*, ed. Jean Seznec and Jean Adhemar (Oxford, 1963), pp. 228–9. I am grateful to Janine Barrier of the Sorbonne for her introductions to French *ruinistes* at a memorable dinner in Paris.

For the Hugos at No. 18 Rue des Petits-Augustins see Graham Robb, *Victor Hugo* ( 1997).

## VIII *Self-portrait in Ruins*

See *Visions of Ruin* (1999), which includes 'Crude Hints Towards a History of My House' transcribed and interpreted by Helen Dorey. Daniel Abramson's discussion of the 'Bank in Ruins' is in his PhD thesis on *The Building of the Bank of England 1731–1833* (Harvard, 1993), pp. 425–9. For more on the tomb and its relationship to posterity, see the article by R. Bowdler and C. Woodward in *Journal of the Society of Architectural Historians* (1999).

## IX *The Ozymandias complex*

For Thomas Coryate and his *Crudities* see Michael Strachan, *Thomas Coryate* (Oxford, 1982). Like Macaulay (1953), Strachan discusses the confusion between Priam's Troy and Alexandria Troias, a misunderstanding which continued into the nineteenth century owing to the impreciseness of ancient geographers such as Strabo and the absence of any visible remains at the real site. Julian (332–63) visited Troy before he became Emperor, and his description of Troy is in *The Works of the Emperor Julian*, translated by Wilmer Cave Wright (Cambridge and London, 1990).

The continuing potency of religious imagery in eighteenth-century England is demonstrated by Terry Friedman in 'The Eighteenth-century Disaster Print' in *Proceedings of the Symposium of the Society of Architectural Historians* (1996), in which he discusses how the destruction of churches by fire or structural collapse was interpreted by reference to the Bible. The revival of Apocalyptic imagery during the French Revolution is explored in David Bindman, 'The English Apocalypse' in *The Apocalypse*, ed. Frances Carey (1990), the catalogue to the British Museum exhibition.

For John Martin's imaginary reconstruction of Babylon see Henrietta McCall, 'Rediscovery and Aftermath' from *The Legacy of Mesopotamia* (Oxford, 1998), pp. 184–213.

H. G. Schenk, 'The Mind of the European Romantics' (1966, pp. 30–45) discusses the foreboding of future ruin in post-Waterloo Europe, and it is he who argues that 'it would seem that the spirit of foreboding has never been so widespread' at that period. Wetzel's vision of goblins was in *Magischer Spiegel* of 1806, while the remarks of the Bavarian scholar Schlichtegroll (p. 32) on Iceland were recorded by Atterbom. Professor David Skilton has suggested in correspondence that we can plot a correlation between political unrest and imagery of ruin throughout the eighteenth and nineteenth centuries in Britain, and will publish this in due course.

The relationship between the Temples of Modern and Ancient Virtue at Stowe and Joseph Addison's dream was revealed by George Clarke in 'Grecian Taste and Gothic Virtue' in *Apollo* (1973), pp. 568–9. For Charlemont on the Acropolis, see the *Travels of Lord Charlemont in Greece and Turkey, 1749*, ed. W. B. Stanford and E. J. Finopoulos (1984), pp. 134–5. His biography is by Cynthia O'Connor (Cork, 1999).

Horace Walpole's letter to Horace Mann, his correspondent in Florence, was written on 24 November 1774.

For Gibbon, see Harold Bond, *The Literary Art of Edward Gibbon* (Oxford, 1960). Ralph Willett, FSA, published *A Description of the Library at Merly in the County of Dorset* (1785); it was Tim Knox who drew attention to the lost peculiarity (*Apollo*, July 2000).

In the catalogue to his controversial exhibition of Richard Wilson at the Tate Gallery (1982), pp. 217–18, David Solkin argued that the artist's Arcadian landscapes were commissioned by conservative landowners who wished to show that ruin was the inevitable consequence of an increase in trade and 'Luxury'. This is true, although one would add that mercantilists such as Ralph Willett also used the same ruins to illustrate their contrary arguments.

As regards America: see Matthew Baigell, *Thomas Cole* (New York, 1981) who proposes the idea of an American School of Catastrophe, represented by the preachers Lyman and Bigelow and Cole's friend William Cullen Bryant whose poems 'The Ages' and 'The Earth' alluded to America's destruction. Cole's thoughts on *The Course of Empire* are recorded in Louis Legrand Noble's nineteenth-century biography, reprinted by the Harvard Press in 1964. Cole never painted New York, a telling point made in a recent exhibition at the Metropolitan Museum which examined New York's conception of itself as an imperial city: *Art and the Empire Setting*. The catalogue is edited by Catherine Voorsanger and John K. Howat (New York, 2000).

Nicholas Biddle's journal was published as *Nicholas Biddle in Greece*, ed. R. A. McNeal (Philadelphia, 1993).

Mussolini's self-projection of himself as a classical hero is discussed in 'Rome Reclaims Its Empire' by Tim Benton in *Art and Power* (1996), pp. 120–39.

X *Dust in the Air Suspended*

The story of the Millennium Cross for Dresden was told by Christopher Kenworthy in the *Telegraph*, 28 November 1998. Michael McMahon's visit to Oradour is in the *Telegraph*, 3 June 2000.

David Fraser Jenkins explains Piper's war in his superb catalogue to the exhibition at the Imperial War Museum: *John Piper: The Forties* (2000). Fraser Jenkins also wrote the catalogue to the 1984 exhibition on Piper at the Tate. Piper's essay 'Pleasing Decay' was in *Buildings and Prospects* (1948).

The final chapter of *Ruins* by Michael Felmingham and Rigby Graham (1972) has very good material on the wartime and post-war period.

Dennis Creffield's paintings of Orford Ness were published in a catalogue to the Connaught Brown exhibition in 1995, with an introduction by Jeremy Musson.


XI *The Novelist, the Fisherman and the Prince*

There are two biographies of Rose Macaulay, by her relation Constance Babington Smith (1972) and by Jane Emery (1991). Babington Smith printed the short story 'Miss Anstruther's Letters' for the first time, and chose extracts from *Pleasure of Ruins* for a book of photographs by Roloff Beny (1964).

David Gilmour has written a biography of Lampedusa which is intelligent, witty, and quite perfect (*The Last Leopard*, 1988). *The Siren* and *Places of My Infancy*, translated by Archibald Colquhoun, were published in *Two Stories and a Memory* (1962).

# Index